Predicate Logic

Predicate Logic

INTRODUCTION TO LOGIC

Howard Pospesel

University of Miami
Coral Gables, Florida

PRENTICE-HALL, INC., Englewood Cliffs, New Jersey

Library of Congress Cataloging in Publication Data

POSPESEL, HOWARD, 1937–
    Predicate logic.

    (Introduction to logic)
    Includes bibliographical references and index.
    1. Predicate (Logic) 2. Proposition (Logic)
3. Logic, Symbolic and mathematical—Problems, exercises, etc. I. Title.
BC181.P638   511'.3   75–30921
ISBN 0-13-486225-2

For Clara

© 1976 by Prentice-Hall, Inc., Englewood Cliffs, New Jersey.

20 19 18 17 16 15 14

Prentice-Hall International (UK) Limited, *London*
Prentice-Hall of Australia Pty. Limited, *Sydney*
Prentice-Hall Canada Inc., *Toronto*
Prentice-Hall Hispanoamericana, S.A., *Mexico*
Prentice-Hall of India Private Limited, *New Delhi*
Prentice-Hall of Japan, Inc., *Tokyo*
Simon & Schuster Asia Pte. Ltd., *Signapore*
Editora Prentice-Hall do Brasil, Ltda., *Rio de Janeiro*

Contents

Student's Preface

I have three aims for this book. The *first* goal is to teach you the vocabulary and grammar of predicate logic so that you will be able to translate the sentences of English (or other natural languages) into the notation of this important branch of symbolic logic. The *second* goal concerns three techniques for evaluating predicate arguments: formal proofs, logic diagrams, and interpretations. I aim to help you become proficient in employing these logical methods. The *third* goal of the book is to develop your ability to identify and assess those predicate arguments you encounter daily as you read books and newspapers, carry on conversations, and watch television. Most of the examples and exercises in the text involve arguments of this everyday variety.

I enjoyed writing the book. If you enjoy studying it (as I hope you will), I think my goals will be achieved.

Teacher's Preface

This text presupposes familiarity with propositional logic and, in particular, acquaintance with the natural-deduction approach to formal proofs in propositional logic.[1] Appendix One contains a review of this material. It will refresh the memory of students previously exposed to the subject, but it is too compact to be fully intelligible to the complete novice.

Predicate logic is developed gradually in this volume, starting with the simplest monadic symbolizations and proceeding through multiple quantification to the logic of relations. Students learn to symbolize *and* evaluate arguments of a given degree of complexity before addressing themselves to the symbolization of more complex problems. This graduated approach has worked well in my logic classes.

The formal-proof system presented here excludes quantifier-introduction rules. I owe the idea to Stephen F. Barker's fine text, *The Elements of Logic*. The main advantages of this system over the more common systems which incorporate quantifier-introduction rules are (1) that the quantifier rules can be stated more simply, and (2) that proofs (although often longer) are generally easier to devise. The set of quantifier rules presented here contains fewer rules than Barker's set. For the sake of deductive completeness, Barker is required to include two (not alto-

---

[1] Natural-deduction proofs are treated extensively in my *Introduction to Logic: Propositional Logic* (Englewood Cliffs, N.J.: Prentice-Hall, Inc., 1974). See Chapters Two through Nine.

gether intuitive) rules which sanction changes in quantifier scope.[2] In my system, these rules are obviated by the adoption of natural-deduction propositional inference rules. An expanded set of inference rules which incorporates quantifier-introduction rules is presented in the second appendix to accommodate teachers who prefer the customary approach.

Most of the examples and exercises center around arguments similar to those encountered by students. The majority of these arguments are *natural*, rather than contrived; many are presented by direct quotation from newspapers and other sources. My purposes in employing natural everyday arguments are (1) to evoke the reader's interest, (2) to counter the common but mistaken view that formal logic is an impractical academic diversion, and (3) to improve the reader's capacity to notice and assess the arguments he encounters. The final chapter explicitly addresses the problems which arise when predicate logic is applied to natural arguments.

[2] See *The Elements of Logic* (2nd ed.; New York: McGraw-Hill Book Company, Inc., 1974), p. 177.

Acknowledgments

William Hanson and David Marans read and criticized the manuscript; their comments led to numerous improvements. David created the crossword puzzle in exercise 220 (Chapter Nine), contributed thirty examples, and helped with proofreading chores. Sherwin Iverson made two valuable suggestions when I first planned the volume. He recommended the inclusion of a chapter on multiple quantification and an appendix presenting an expanded set of proof rules. Production Editor Sandra Di-Somma's careful work improved the book.

These friends contributed exercises: Harold Zellner, Jo Anne Zarowny, Bruce Whitcomb, Fred Westphal, Charles Werner, Bill Webber, Steven Wasserman, Randy Swanson, Linda Stubbs, Marilyn Sher, Linda Schreiber, Miguel Sanabria, James Rachels, Paul Qubeck, Clara Pospesel, Denise Oehmig, Jorge Morales, Virginia Miller, Robert McCleskey, Tommie Kushner, Peter Koujoumis, Stephanie Kazarian, Owen Herring, Elizabeth Hermelee, Jean Henderson, Robert Grier, Caroline Echarte, Robert Dietz, Osvaldo del Rey, Jerry Crangi, Nancy Cain, Edward Braverman, Mark Borgelt, Ray Bielec, Richard Beikirch, and George Bailey.

I am grateful to J. M. Duich for being a professor of turfgrass science, a fact which helped me begin section 5.2.

Predicate Logic

chapter one

Introduction

1.1
Predicate Logic
and Propositional Logic

When my son, Michael, was in the first grade he brought home an issue of *My Weekly Reader*[1] featuring mammals. In large type it proclaimed:

MAMMALS HAVE HAIR

Several photos of mammals followed. Beneath a picture of apes were these words:

Apes have hair. Are apes mammals? Why?

The author of the pictorial essay was encouraging his youthful audience to reason as follows:

[1]*My Weekly Reader Picture Reader*, Vol. 49, Issue 1 (September 15, 1971), pp. 2a–2d.

Mammals have hair.

Apes have hair.

Therefore, apes are mammals.

Let's call this the "ape" argument.

During that school year Michael was given a standardized intelligence test which included this item:

> *All school buses are yellow. The bus that goes downtown is green. Greyhound buses are blue and silver.*

3. *What can you tell from this story?*
   a. *School buses cannot go downtown.*
   b. *A green bus is not a school bus.*
   c. *Yellow buses do not look good.*
   d. *Some school buses are blue and silver.*

The grading key identified (b) as the proper answer. (Michael chose this answer.) Pretty clearly, the test constructor was inviting students to reason:

All school buses are yellow.

A green bus is not yellow. [Unstated premise]

Thus, a green bus is not a school bus.

We will call this the "bus" argument.

One of these arguments is valid; that is, its conclusion follows with necessity from its premises.[2] The other argument is invalid; its conclusion does not follow. Which one is valid? Why is the other argument invalid? *Predicate logic* is a discipline which provides techniques for answering these questions.[3] Of course, it also enables us to answer similar questions about arguments which are much more complex than the "ape" and "bus" inferences—arguments such as this one advanced by Fran Tarkenton before Super Bowl VI:

[As Dallas is facing Miami] either Roger Staubach or Bob Griese will win a championship.

Both men are scrambling quarterbacks.

It follows that the axiom that a scrambling quarterback will never win a championship is mistaken.[4]

---

[2]Another (equivalent) definition of *validity:* a valid argument is one having a form such that it is impossible that its premises are all true and its conclusion false.

[3]The "ape" and "bus" arguments are assessed in section 6.2.

[4]This argument is exercise 41 in Chapter Five.

So far I have indicated that predicate logic is a branch of logic which can be applied to the arguments displayed in the preceding three paragraphs. To achieve a better understanding of what predicate logic is we contrast it with *propositional logic*. Propositional logic is the logic of the five expressions 'not', 'and', 'or', 'if . . . then', and 'if and only if'. This volume presupposes a knowledge of propositional logic. The first appendix provides a review of this branch of logic and describes the specific techniques of propositional logic that are used in the book. If your knowledge of this part of logic has become "rusty," it will be to your advantage to study Appendix One before addressing Chapter Two.

The "ape" and "bus" arguments may be symbolized in propositional logic as follows:

(ape) $B, C \vdash D$ B = Mammals have hair

C = Apes have hair

D = Apes are mammals

(bus) $E, \sim F \vdash \sim H$ E = All school buses are yellow

F = Some green buses are yellow

H = Some green buses are school buses

If these two symbolized arguments are assessed with the techniques of propositional logic, the verdict "invalid" will be rendered twice. This is hardly surprising in view of the fact that no capital letter occurs more than once in either symbolized argument. In each English argument there are several recurring elements; for example, the term 'mammals' occurs twice in the "ape" argument. With the exception of the term 'not' in the "bus" argument, the recurring elements are *not* represented in the propositional symbolization; and they are not represented because they are not propositions (statements) or statement connectives. The feeling that these symbolizations ignore important aspects of the English arguments is strengthened by the following consideration. One of the arguments expressed in English is valid. Neither of the symbolized arguments is valid. Therefore, at least one of the symbolizations is inadequate. In fact, both symbolizations are inadequate; both ignore aspects of the English arguments that are crucial for their validity or invalidity.

The English arguments contain double occurrences of general terms (which we shall call *predicates*), expressions such as 'apes' and 'yellow'. A logic which is adequate to the task of evaluating such arguments must be capable of representing these general terms. Because general terms are not statements or statement connectives, they cannot be represented by propositional logic. Predicate logic, by contrast, contains the symbolic equipment for representing general terms. In propositional logic simple statements are the smallest units of analysis. In predicate logic simple statements are analyzed into parts (some of which are general terms). Thus, predicate logic provides a deeper analysis than does propositional logic. For some arguments the latter branch of logic is an adequate tool of analysis, but for other arguments it is insufficient. Many arguments falling beyond the scope of propositional logic can be treated successfully in predicate logic. The "ape" and "bus" inferences are two such arguments. We can define 'predicate logic' roughly as the logic of general terms. Your conception of the nature and scope of this branch of logic will become clearer as you work through the book.

Predicate logic and propositional logic are intimately connected. All of the symbols of propositional logic appear in the formulas of predicate logic, and all of the propositional inference rules are employed in constructing formal proofs in predicate logic. Obviously it is absolutely essential that a person studying this book know the logic of propositions. In the chapters which follow, we shall develop a formal system of predicate logic by grafting new "branches" onto the "trunk" of propositional logic. The symbols of predicate logic will be added to our vocabulary in Chapters Two and Ten. We will add just three predicate inference rules to the eighteen propositional rules listed on pages 203 and 204. Two rules are introduced in Chapter Three and one in Chapter Four.

chapter two

Symbolization

2.1
Singular Statements

Many English sentences can be viewed as consisting of two parts: an expression which is used to refer to an individual, and an expression which is used to ascribe some property to the individual. Let's call expressions of the former sort *singular terms* and expressions of the latter kind *predicates.* Sentences composed of singular terms and predicates are known as *singular statements.* Some examples:

SINGULAR STATEMENT	SINGULAR TERM	PREDICATE
Ted Kennedy is a Democrat.	Ted Kennedy	is a Democrat
David's tumor is an acoustic neuroma.	David's tumor	is an acoustic neuroma
She sings poorly.	she	sings poorly
The first man to walk on the Moon is American.	the first man to walk on the Moon	is American

The key characteristic of a singular term is that it is customarily used to refer to an individual. I use *individual* broadly, counting not only people but pets, rivers, rocks, cities, planets, numbers, and so on as individuals. Singular terms are expressions that function like proper nouns, but the concept is a logical, not a grammatical one. Singular terms may be proper nouns ('Shakespeare'), pronouns ('he'), or noun phrases ('David's tumor', 'the janitor'). In predicate logic we abbreviate singular terms with lower-case letters of the alphabet from a through w (the letters x, y, and z are reserved for another use which is explained in the next section). Normally the letter chosen as an abbreviation will be the first letter of a prominent word occurring in the singular term; for example, j will abbreviate 'the janitor'. Let's call the letters that abbreviate singular terms *names*.

A predicate or general term is an expression which may be used to ascribe a property (such as *being fat*) to an individual or to assert that several individuals stand in some relationship (like *hating*). At present we will concentrate on property predicates, postponing our treatment of relational predicates until Chapter Ten. Predicates may be composed of various parts of speech. Some examples:

PREDICATE	PART OF SPEECH
sleeps	verb
sleeps poorly	verb + adverb
speaks German	verb + noun
is greedy	copula[1] + adjective
is a Texan	copula + noun phrase

It will become clear as we proceed that our concept of "predicate" does not correspond exactly to the grammarian's notion. Predicates are abbreviated in our logic by capital letters. The letter selected will usually be the first letter of one of the words comprising the predicate; for example, T will abbreviate 'is a Texan'. We call the letters that abbreviate English predicates *predicate letters* (or just *predicates*).

To symbolize an affirmative singular statement in the notation of predicate logic, we write the capital which abbreviates the predicate followed by the lower-case letter which serves as the abbreviation of the singular term. S1 is symbolized by F1.

(S1)   David's <u>tumor</u> is an acoustic NEUROMA.

(F1)   Nt

[1]A copula is a word or expression (such as a form of the verb 'to be') that links the subject of a sentence with its grammatical predicate without asserting action.

I use two conventions for designating abbreviations: (1) underlining the word in the singular term whose first letter will serve as the name, and (2) printing entirely in capitals the word in the predicate whose first letter will be the predicate letter. Notice that the predicate-first order displayed by F1 is not the standard pattern of English sentences.

Some singular statements are negative; S2 is an instance.

> (S2) <u>Shakespeare</u> was not GAY.

A negative singular statement is symbolized as the negation of an affirmative one. S2 is symbolized by F2.

> (F2) ~Gs

This is our first example of the use of a symbol of propositional logic in a predicate-logic wff (well-formed formula). Is S3 affirmative or negative? Should it be symbolized by F4 or F5?

> (S3) Baruch's first <u>argument</u> is invalid.
>
> (F4) Ia [*I* abbreviates 'is invalid'.]
>
> (F5) ~Va [*V* abbreviates 'is valid'.]

Considering S3 out of context, our decision is arbitrary. When S3 is viewed as part of some argument, one symbolization may be preferable.

2.2
General Statements: *I* and *O*

Let's define a *singular statement* as a statement containing one or more singular terms. We shall call a statement that has no singular terms a *general statement*. (Does it follow from these definitions that every statement is either singular or general? Do the definitions imply that no statement is both?) A singular statement mentions one or more specified individuals; a general statement concerns individuals of certain kinds or types but does not name any specific individual. S1 is a sample general statement:

> (S1) Some rabbis are Japanese.

S1 concerns rabbis but it refers to no specific rabbi. In this regard S1 contrasts sharply with the singular statement S2.

> (S2) Hiroshi Okamoto is a rabbi.

Ever since Aristotle developed syllogistic logic[2] 2300 years ago, logicians have been especially interested in general statements which exhibit any of four simple forms. These forms are given in the following table.

Four Basic General Statement-Forms

FORM	EXAMPLE	LABEL	CODE LETTER
All $\mathcal{D}$ are $\mathcal{E}$	All pines are conifers.	universal affirmative	A
No $\mathcal{D}$ are $\mathcal{E}$	No conservatives are nudists.	universal negative	E
Some $\mathcal{D}$ are $\mathcal{E}$	Some rabbis are Japanese.	particular affirmative	I
Some $\mathcal{D}$ are not $\mathcal{E}$	Some psychologists are not atheists.	particular negative	O

The labels and code letters for the four statement-forms in this table have been employed for many centuries. I shall use the code letters but not the labels. In the remainder of this section we concentrate on statements of types *I* and *O*. Section 2.3 treats statements of types *A* and *E*.

In predicate logic any statement exhibiting one of the four basic general statement-forms is regarded as containing two predicates. Consider again S1.

(S1)   Some rabbis are Japanese.

Without altering the content of S1 we can rephrase it as S1′.

(S1′)   There exists at least one individual who *is a rabbi* and *is Japanese*.

The two predicates are brought to the surface in S1′. They can be symbolized as *R* and *J*. Two other symbols of predicate logic are required to fully symbolize S1′: the *variable* and the *existential quantifier*. We employ the lower-case letters *x*, *y*, and *z* as variables. If a wff requires more than three variables, we can form additional ones with the prime mark (thus *x*′). Until we reach Chapter Ten, however, we will manage with

---

[2] Syllogistic logic is described briefly in section 4.1.

just one variable: x. The variable is a symbolic device for cross-reference. The closest analogue in English to the variable is the pronoun. The existential quantifier consists of an inverted E followed by a variable, the whole enclosed in parentheses. '$(\exists x)$' is read *there exists an x such that*.

We now have the machinery required to symbolize S1' (and thus S1).

There exists at least one individual who	is a rabbi	and	is Japanese
$(\exists x)$	(Rx	&	Jx)

So we reach F1 as our symbolization of S1.

(F1) $(\exists x)(Rx \,\&\, Jx)$

F1 may be read *There exists an x such that x is a rabbi and x is Japanese.* Every I statement is symbolized in similar fashion. The purpose of the second pair of parentheses in F1 will be explained in section 5.1. It is sufficient at present to note that each wff symbolizing an I statement (or an O, A or E) has a left-hand parenthesis after the quantifier and a right-hand one as concluding symbol.

I statements can be disguised in different English garments. All of the statements in this list are regarded as I statements by logicians and are symbolized by F1.

At least one rabbi is Japanese.

Rabbis are sometimes Japanese.

There are rabbis who are Japanese.

Many rabbis are Japanese.

Rabbis who are Japanese do exist.

The list is not exhaustive.

English sentences of the I-variety exhibit *vagueness* and *ambiguity*. As an example of the former, consider again S1:

(S1) Some rabbis are Japanese.

How many Japanese rabbis must there be if S1 is to express a truth? There is no definite answer to this question, if it is a question about English usage. However, in deciding to paraphrase S1 as S1', we have stipulated (for the purposes of logic) that *one* Japanese rabbi is sufficient for the truth of S1.

(S1') There exists at least one individual who is a rabbi and is Japanese.

As an example of the *ambiguity* of sentences of the *I*-type consider S3:

> (S3) Some dogs are mammals.

Is S3 true? One who utters S3 may be intending to claim S4, or he may be making the stronger claim expressed by S5.

> (S4) At *least* some dogs are mammals.
>
> (S5) Some dogs (and at *most* some dogs) are mammals.

S4 is true, S5 is false. In logic, we will regard S3 as equivalent to S4; so, we count S3 a truth.

Having learned how to symbolize *I* statements, it is an easy step to the symbolization of *O* statements. S6 serves as an example.

> (S6) Some psychologists are not atheists.

S6 may be rephrased as S6′, which in turn is symbolized by F6.

> (S6′) There exists an *x* such that *x* is a PSYCHOLOGIST but *x* is not an ATHEIST.
>
> (F6) (∃x)(Px & ~Ax)

Every *O* statement may be symbolized in this way. Notice that the tilde is properly located after the ampersand. Neither of the following wffs symbolizes S6.

> (F7) (∃x)~(Px & Ax)
>
> (F8) ~(∃x)(Px & Ax)

F7 and F8 symbolize S7 and S8, respectively. Neither S7 nor S8 is equivalent to S6.

> (S7) Someone is not both a psychologist and an atheist.
>
> (S8) It is false that there is a psychologist who is an atheist.

O statements can be expressed in English in various ways, for example:

> At least one psychologist is not an atheist.
>
> There are psychologists who aren't atheists.
>
> Not all psychologists are atheists.

Each of these sentences is correctly symbolized by F6. This list does not include all of the *O*-variants.

EXERCISE

1. Symbolize these statements using the suggested abbreviations. Each statement is either singular, an *I*, or an *O*.

   (a) Three is a PRIME.

   (b) *(Newspaper)* "Some INDIANS do have BEARDS."

   *(c) Some statements that we are JUSTIFIED in believing are not TRUE. (*Jx =x* is a statement that we are justified in believing)

   *(d) Norman Mailer isn't a DENTIST.

   (e) There is a NEGRO Supreme Court JUSTICE.

   (f) *(Newspaper ad)* "Not all JEWS are FOR Jesus." (*Fx =x* is for Jesus)

   (g) GOLDEN FAUCETS exist.

   (h) The pilot who bailed out of that Egyptian jet is not DARK haired.

   *(i) *(Scientific American article)* "Many BIRDS can fly at high ALTITUDES." (*Ax =x* can fly at high altitudes)

   (j) *(Children's book)* "There are many PEOPLE who cannot TELL the difference between an alligator who is smiling and an alligator who is not smiling." (*Px = x* is a person, *Tx = x* can tell the difference between an alligator who is smiling and an alligator who is not smiling)

2.3
General Statements: *A* and *E*

The introduction of one more symbol of predicate logic—the *universal quantifier*—will enable us to symbolize *A* and *E* statements. (No additional symbols will be needed until Chapter Ten.) The universal quantifier consists of a variable flanked by parentheses. '(x)' is read *for any x*. How shall we symbolize S1?

(S1)   All pines are conifers.

As a first step we paraphrase S1 as S1′.

(S1′)   For any individual, if it is a PINE, then it is a CONIFER.

S1′ is composed exclusively of predicates and expressions that correspond to symbols in our logical vocabulary. We symbolize S1′ (and hence S1) with F1.

*Solutions (or partial solutions) to starred problems are provided in Appendix Three.

(F1) (x)(Px → Cx)

F1 is read *For any x, if x is a pine, then x is a conifer.* Any A statement may be symbolized in this fashion.

Why employ an arrow rather than an ampersand; why not symbolize S1 with F2?

(F2) (x)(Px & Cx)

F2 is read *For any x, x is a pine and x is a conifer.* It symbolizes S2 which, of course, does not have the same content as S1.

(S2) Everything is a pine and a conifer.

A statements (or sentences equivalent to such statements) occur very often in natural languages. It is not surprising then that English offers many ways of expressing A statements. Some are included in this list.

> Every pine is a conifer.
>
> Each pine is a conifer.
>
> Each and every pine is a conifer.
>
> Any pine is a conifer.
>
> A pine is a conifer.
>
> Pines are all conifers.
>
> Pines are always conifers.
>
> Pines are conifers.

Each of these sentences is properly symbolized by F1. Notice that the order of the predicates in an A wff is crucial. Switching the predicates of F1 yields F3.

(F3) (x)(Cx → Px)

But F3 does not represent S1 or any of the variants listed above. F3 symbolizes (the false) S3.

(S3) All conifers are pines.

Two A variants involving the expressions 'only' and 'none but' are troublesome and deserve special treatment. S4 and S5 serve as representatives.

(S4) Only males are National Football League players.

(S5) None but males are NFL players.

Let's begin with S4. S4 has the same content as S6:

(S6)   All NFL PLAYERS are MALES.

We can formulate this principle for transforming "only" statements into standard *A* statements:

Only $\mathcal{D}$ **are** $\mathcal{E}$ = **All** $\mathcal{E}$ **are** $\mathcal{D}$

As S4 and S6 are equivalent, both may be symbolized by F6.

(F6)   (x)(Px → Mx)

People are often confused by "only" statements. For example, some may believe that S4 has the same content as S7.

(S4)   Only males are NFL players.
(S7)   All males are NFL players.

We can prove conclusively that S4 and S7 are not equivalent. S4 is true while S7 is false. If they were logically equivalent,[3] they would have the same truth value. So they are not logically equivalent. We can also prove that S4 and S6 are equivalent. Consider these four statements:

(S6)   All NFL players are males.
       No NFL players are nonmales.
       No nonmales are NFL players.
(S4)   Only males are NFL players.

Each of the first three statements in this list is logically equivalent to the statement directly beneath it. Therefore, S4 is logically equivalent to S6. (This argument is assessed in section 11.1)

Having mastered the treatment of "only" statements, we can handle "none but" statements easily. This principle suffices:

None but $\mathcal{D}$ *are* $\mathcal{E}$ = *Only* $\mathcal{D}$ *are* $\mathcal{E}$

S5 is equivalent to S4, and therefore to S6.

(S5)   None but males are NFL players.
(S4)   Only males are NFL players.
(S6)   All NFL players are males.

Of the four basic general statement-forms, only the *E* form remains to be treated. S9 is a representative *E* statement:

(S9)   No conservatives are nudists.

[3]Two statements are logically equivalent if and only if it is logically impossible for one to be true and the other false.

We can paraphrase S9 in a way which employs two predicates and certain other readily symbolized expressions.

(S9') For any x, if x is a CONSERVATIVE, then x is not a NUDIST.

S9' (and also S9) is symbolized by F9.

(F9) (x)(Cx → ~Nx)

The tilde is properly located after the arrow (as in F9). None of the following wffs symbolizes S9:

~(x)(Cx → Nx)
(x)~(Cx → Nx)
(x)(~Cx → Nx)

There are many ways of expressing E statements in English; here are some:

Conservatives are never nudists.
Conservatives are not nudists.
Conservatives aren't nudists.
No one is both a conservative and a nudist.
Conservative nudists don't exist.
There are no conservative nudists.

F9 symbolizes each of these sentences.

An introduction-to-philosophy midterm I graded contained this sentence:

(S10) All events are not caused.

Had S10 not been imbedded in an essay, I would not have known whether the student was asserting S11 or S12.

(S11) No events are caused.
(S12) Some events are not caused.

Sentences of the form *All $\mathcal{D}$ are not $\mathcal{E}$* are ambiguous. (Distinguish this form from the unambiguous form *Not all $\mathcal{D}$ are $\mathcal{E}$*, which was discussed in section 2.2.) In deciding whether to view a sentence such as S10 as an E or an O statement, we must pay attention to intonation (for speech) and to the context in which the sentence occurs. A person who dislikes unnecessary ambiguity will avoid formulating sentences of S10's type.

The national high school mathematics examination for 1975 included this item:

> If the statement "All shirts in this store are on sale" is false, then which of the following statements must be true?
>
> I.   All shirts in this store are not on sale.
> II. There is some shirt in this store not on sale.
> III. No shirt in this store is on sale.
> IV. Not all shirts in this store are on sale.
>
> (A) II only   (C) I and III only   (E) I, II and IV only
> (B) IV only   (D) II and IV only

Sentences II and IV are *O* statements. They must be true if the given statement ("All shirts in this store are on sale") is false. Sentence III is an *E* statement. It may be false even if the given statement is false. Sentence number I is an ambiguous sentence of the type just discussed. It can be read as an *E* or an *O* statement. (Read the sentence several times stressing different components.) How one reads sentence number I will determine the answer one selects [(D) or (E)]. I think the test item is poor.[4]

2.4
Résumé

The symbols of predicate logic introduced in this chapter are listed in the following table.

Symbols of Predicate Logic

SYMBOL NAME	SYMBOLS	READING
predicates	A, B, . . ., Z	
names	a, b, . . ., w	
variable	x	
universal quantifier	(x)	for any x
existential quantifier	(∃x)	there exists an x such that

[4] The test constructors might argue that answer (E) is excluded precisely because sentence number I is ambiguous. That sentence *might* be understood in such a way that it *could* be false while the given statement is false. If they view the item in this way, they have concocted a very tricky question.

With the aid of these symbols together with some of the symbols of propositional logic we have been able to symbolize six common kinds of statements. Representative symbolizations are presented in the next table.

Six Standard Statements Symbolized

TYPE	EXAMPLE	SYMBOLIZATION
singular affirmative	David's <u>tumor</u> is an acoustic NEUROMA.	Nt
singular negative	<u>Shakespeare</u> was not GAY.	~Gs
A	All PINES are CONIFERS.	(x)(Px → Cx)
E	No CONSERVATIVES are NUDISTS.	(x)(Cx → ~Nx)
I	Some RABBIS are JAPANESE.	(∃x)(Rx & Jx)
O	Some PSYCHOLOGISTS are not ATHEISTS.	(∃x)(Px & ~Ax)

In Chapters Three and Four we will examine arguments composed of statements of these six kinds (and their negations).

EXERCISES

2. Symbolize these statements using the suggested abbreviations. Each statement belongs to one of the six types discussed in the chapter.

   (a) *(Newspaper)* "All great SPRINTERS are great WEIGHTLIFTERS."

   *(b) *(Daniel Berrigan)* "No PRINCIPLE is WORTH the sacrifice of a single human life." (Wx = x is worth the sacrifice of a human life)

   (c) *(John 3:20)* "Every one who does EVIL HATES the light." (Ex = x does evil)

   (d) *(Children's book)* "Some WHALES have TEETH."

   (e) GOURMETS don't ORDER well-done steaks. (Ox = x orders well-done steaks)

   (f) *(Label)* "Each TABLET SUPPLIES 3 1/3 times the minimum daily adult requirement of Vitamin C."

   (g) *(Comicstrip)* "Anybody who RACES horses has got to BELIEVE in miracles."

(h) Daniel <u>Berrigan</u> is MARRIED.

(i) Many of the world's PHILOSOPHERS are ALIVE today.

(j) *(Charlie Brown)* "To KNOW me is to LOVE me." ($Kx = x$ knows Charlie, $Lx = x$ loves Charlie)

*(k) *(Mummy movie)* "He who defiles an EGYPTIAN tomb, DIES." ($Ex = x$ defiles an Egyptian tomb)

(l) *(Newspaper)* "All loitering LAWS are unconstitutional." ($Cx = x$ is constitutional)

*(m) *("Papa Doc" Duvalier)* "Only the GODS can take POWER from me." ($Px = x$ can take power from Duvalier)

(n) *(W. C. Fields)* "A thing worth HAVING is a thing worth CHEATING for." ($Hx = x$ is worth having, $Cx = x$ is worth cheating for)

(o) Some WATERBIRDS lack OIL glands. ($Ox = x$ has oil glands)

*(p) *(Catch-22)* "What's good for M & M ENTERPRISES is good for the COUNTRY." ($Ex = x$ is good for M & M Enterprises, $Cx = x$ is good for the country)

(q) *(Newspaper)* "Not everyone who TRAINS WINS."

(r) *(Samuel Johnson)* "No man but a LUNATIC would be a SAILOR."

(s) *(Newspaper)* "There were no PRESIDENTS of the United States who were JEHOVAH'S Witnesses."

(t) *(Boswell)* "Those who would endeavor to extirpate EVIL from the world know LITTLE of human nature." ($Ex = x$ endeavors to extirpate evil from the world, $Lx = x$ knows little of human nature)

(u) <u>Kentucky</u> didn't SECEDE.

(v) YEOMEN are all PETTY officers.

(w) *(Erskine Caldwell)* "You cannot be both a good SOCIALIZER and a good WRITER."

*(x) *(Movie title)* "LONELY are the BRAVE."

(y) *(TV commercial)* "If it's BORDEN'S, it's got to be GOOD." ($Bx = x$ is a Borden's product)

3. Translate each wff into a colloquial English sentence using the dictionary provided.

  n = Ralph Nader

  $Cx = x$ is a consumer advocate

  $Rx = x$ is a Republican

  $Ax = x$ is an activist

(a) Cn

(b) ~Rn

*(c) (x)(Cx → Ax)

(d) (x)(Ax → Cx)

(e) (x)(Rx → ~Ax)

(f) (∃x)(Rx & Cx)

(g) (∃x)(Rx & ~Cx)

(h) (∃x)(Cx & ~Rx)

Note: The next two exercises are more difficult than any of the preceding ones; they require ingenuity. If you enjoy a challenge, you will want to tackle them. There are challenging problems in most of the exercise sets in the volume. To distinguish them from the other exercises, I have (1) marked them with the word 'CHALLENGING' and (2) employed a separate numbering system (beginning with '200').

200. (CHALLENGING) Symbolize these statements using the suggested abbreviations. Each statement belongs to one of the six types discussed in the chapter.

(a) *(Radio commercial)* "SMOKE and MAKE your doctor rich." ($Sx = x$ smokes, $Mx = x$ makes his doctor rich)

(b) *(Newspaper)* "The only horses who broke down on SAF-T-TURF were those who had already BROKEN down." ($Sx = x$ is a horse who broke down on Saf-T-Turf, $Bx = x$ is a horse who has broken down before)

(Note: Distinguish 'The only 𝒟 are ℰ' from 'Only 𝒟 are ℰ'. Can you formulate a translation principle for statements such as b?)

(c) A SALESMAN was MURDERED.

(d) *(Parental dictum)* "Nobody GOES to the Carvel store unless he cleans his PLATE." ($Gx = x$ goes to the Carvel store, $Px = x$ cleans his plate)

(e) *(TV commercial)* "BAYER is all ASPIRIN." ($Bx = x$ is a molecular particle of a Bayer tablet, $Ax = x$ is aspirin)

(f) *(TV commercial)* "Bayer is only aspirin." (Use dictionary for e.)

(g) *(Walt Kelley)* "There's nothing but LOSERS in a WAR." ($Wx = x$ is involved in a war)

(h) *(Camus)* "No one can be HAPPY without causing harm to OTHERS." ($Hx = x$ is happy, $Ox = x$ harms others)

(i) *(Milton)* "Nothing of all these evils hath BEFALLEN me but justly." ($Bx = x$ is an evil that has befallen me, $Dx = x$ is an evil I deserve)

(j) "Show me a man who greets each sunrise with a big SMILE, and I'll show you a man with TAN gums." ($Sx = x$ is a man who greets each sunrise with a big smile, $Tx = x$ is a man with tan gums)

March 26, 1974. By permission of John
Hart and Field Enterprises, Inc.

201. (CHALLENGING) Symbolize these statements, employing the suggested
abbreviations.

(a) All PARENTS are ELIGIBLE.

(b) Any parent is eligible.

(c) Not all parents are eligible.

(d) Not any parent is eligible.

(e) If all parents are eligible, Dean is.

(f) If any parent is eligible, Dean is.

chapter three

Proofs

3.1
Universal Quantifier Out

Austin was certain he was dead; his psychiatrist endeavored to convince him otherwise. The doctor got Austin to admit that dead men don't bleed, whereupon the doctor grabbed a scalpel and nicked his patient's arm. Watching blood flow from the cut, Austin exclaimed, "By Jove, dead men *do* bleed!" This yarn revolves about two arguments, one advanced by the psychiatrist, the other by his patient. The psychiatrist's argument:

> DEAD men don't BLEED.
>
> <u>Austin</u> bleeds.
>
> Hence, Austin is not dead.

This argument consists of an E statement and two singular statements. It is symbolized readily.

$$(x)(Dx \rightarrow \sim Bx), Ba \vdash \sim Da$$

Austin found this argument unconvincing and advanced one of his own, which was a criticism of the first premise of the doctor's inference. Austin's argument:

I am bleeding.

I am dead.

Therefore, it is false that dead men don't bleed.

This argument is composed of two singular statements and the denial of an *E* statement. It is symbolized:

Ba, Da ⊢ ~(x)(Dx → ~Bx)

One of the main concerns of any branch of logic is to develop instruments for establishing the validity of arguments. In this chapter and the next, I present a device for establishing the validity of predicate arguments such as the two considered in the preceding paragraph — the method of *formal proof*.[1] Completing a formal proof for an argument demonstrates that it is valid. In constructing proofs we shall make constant use of the eighteen propositional inference rules listed on pages 203 and 204. We will also require three rules permitting us to manipulate universal and existential quantifiers. I present these quantifier rules in Chapters Three and Four.

Some definitions prepare the way for these rules.[2] First, we define a *universal quantification* as a wff beginning with a universal quantifier. F1 is a universal quantification; F2 is not.

(F1) (x)(Cx → Dx)

(F2) ~(x)(Cx → Dx)

Now we define an *instance* of a universal quantification as a wff which results from (a) deleting the quantifier and (b) replacing each of the remaining occurrences of the variable by the same name. F3 and F4 are instances of F1.

(F3) Ca → Da

(F4) Cb → Db

F5 and F6 are not instances of F1. Why?[3]

---

[1] The concept of "formal proof" is discussed in Appendix One.

[2] These definitions are sufficient for present purposes but will need to be altered in sections 5.1 and 11.1.

[3] F5: *a* and *b* are not the same name. F6: *y* is not a name but a variable.

(F5) Ca → Db

(F6) Cy → Dy

The first predicate inference rule:

The Universal Quantifier Out Rule (UO): From a universal quantification derive any instance of it.

This rule (as well as the other predicate inference rules introduced in the following sections) is correctly applied to *whole* lines only. The standard assumption-dependence principle applies to each rule. (That is, the statement derived depends on all of the assumptions on which the premise of the step depends.) To illustrate the use of the UO Rule I will construct a proof for the psychiatrist's argument, which was symbolized:

(x)(Dx → ~Bx), Ba ⊢ ~Da

The proof is not long:

(1) (x)(Dx → ~Bx)   A

(2) Ba   A

(3) Da → ~Ba   1 UO

(4) Ba → ~Da   3 CN

(5) ~Da   4,2 →O

Line 3 is an instance of the universal quantification on line 1; hence the UO Rule was correctly applied in deriving line 3. The name I chose to "instantiate" to on line 3 was *a*. I selected *a* because it occurred in the second premise and the conclusion of the symbolized argument. Had I instantiated to any other name on line 3 I would have been unable to complete the proof. The Arrow Out step on line 5 can be made only if the antecedent of line 4 is identical with line 2; thus line 4 must contain *a*.

The proof above is not the only correct proof which can be devised for the psychiatrist's argument. For example, instead of employing the Rules of Contraposition and Arrow Out, I might have used Double Negation (from line 2) and Modus Tollens. For any valid predicate argument there are multiple correct proofs. A practical corollary: if a proof you construct for a starred exercise differs from the proof given in the third appendix, your proof may yet be correct.

Either of two questions may have occurred to you: *Why is the UO Rule sound?* and *Why is it needed?* Let's consider these questions in turn. The rule is based on the elementary logical principle that what is true of *every* individual is true of *any named* individual. Thus if it is true of every number that it has a successor, then it is true of 17 that it has a successor. A universal quantification represents a claim about every individual; an instance of that universal quantification represents the same claim applied to a specified (named) individual. The universal quantification on line 1 of the above proof says of every individual that if it is dead, then it does not bleed. The instance on line 3 says of Austin that if he is dead, then he does not bleed.

Why is the UO Rule needed? The rule allows us to derive from a universal quantification a wff which essentially belongs to propositional logic; it allows us to derive a wff to which we can apply the propositional inference rules. Contrast lines 1 and 3 of the above proof. The main symbol in line 1 is the universal quantifier, not the arrow; line 1 is a quantification, not a conditional. Thus a propositional rule such as Contraposition cannot be applied correctly to line 1. By contrast, the main symbol in line 3 is the arrow; line 3 is a conditional. Contraposition can be applied to that line. So the purpose of the UO Rule is to allow us to derive from universal quantifications wffs which lend themselves to manipulation by the inference rules of propositional logic.

For a second illustration of the use of the UO Rule I will construct a proof for Austin's argument. This inference was symbolized:

Ba, Da $\vdash \sim$(x)(Dx $\rightarrow \sim$Bx)

A proof:

1	(1)	Ba	A
2	(2)	Da	A
3	(3)	(x)(Dx $\rightarrow \sim$Bx)	PA
3	(4)	Da $\rightarrow \sim$Ba	3 UO
2,3	(5)	$\sim$Ba	4,2 $\rightarrow$O
1,2,3	(6)	Ba & $\sim$Ba	1,5 &I
1,2	(7)	$\sim$(x)(Dx $\rightarrow \sim$Bx)	3–6 $\sim$I

We have no rule of inference which sanctions *introducing* a universal quantifier into a proof; we have only a rule for eliminating such a quantifier.[4] This fact plus the fact that the conclusion of the argument is a negation dictated a Tilde In strategy; so a provisional assumption of the conclusion less its tilde was made on line 3. When a standard contradiction[5] was reached on line 6, an application of Tilde In finished the proof.

The employment of a provisional assumption in the proof above prompted the inclusion (on the left) of an assumption-dependence column. This column makes it evident that line 7, the argument's conclusion, depends only on the original assumptions and not on the provi-

---

[4] Some systems of predicate logic contain rules for introducing quantifiers. See, for example, Appendix Two.

[5] A *standard contradiction* is a conjunction whose right conjunct is the negation of the left conjunct.

sional assumption. For the sake of convenience I propose that in certain proofs we dispense with the assumption-dependence column. Let's define a *standard Tilde proof* as a proof containing one provisional assumption which is discharged on the last line of the proof by a step of Tilde In or Tilde Out. We will omit the assumption-dependence column in all standard Tilde proofs. The primary purpose of the column is to ensure that the final line in the proof depends on no provisional assumption. In a standard Tilde proof the sole provisional assumption will always be discharged by the final proof step; hence, the column is unnecessary. This change in procedure effects a substantial economy, since most of the proofs we will construct in predicate logic are standard Tilde proofs. We will continue to utilize the assumption-dependence column in proofs which are not standard Tilde proofs but which contain provisional assumptions.

For a final example of the use of the UO Rule we turn to the lyrics of the rock opera "Jesus Christ Superstar." Pilate addresses Jesus:

> *Since you come from Galilee then you need not come to me. You're Herod's race! You're Herod's case!*[6]

Pilate is evidently reasoning in this way:

> Jesus is from GALILEE. Galileans are of Herod's RACE. Anyone of Herod's race comes UNDER his jurisdiction. Thus, Jesus is under Herod's jurisdiction.

Symbolized:

$$Gj, (x)(Gx \rightarrow Rx), (x)(Rx \rightarrow Ux) \vdash Uj$$

A proof:

(1)	Gj	A
(2)	$(x)(Gx \rightarrow Rx)$	A
(3)	$(x)(Rx \rightarrow Ux)$	A
(4)	$Gj \rightarrow Rj$	2 UO
(5)	$Rj \rightarrow Uj$	3 UO
(6)	Rj	4,1 →O
(7)	Uj	5,6 →O

---

[6] "Pilot and Christ" from *Jesus Christ Superstar A Rock Opera* by Andrew Lloyd Webber and Tim Rice. Copyright © 1970 by Leeds Music Ltd. London, England. Sole selling agent, Leeds Music Corporation, 445 Park Ave., New York, N.Y., for North, Central and South America. Used by permission. All rights reserved.

EXERCISES

4. Complete the following proofs. Every assumption has been identified.
Assumption-dependence columns are not required.

(a) (1) Ab   A
    (2) (x)(Ax → Cx)   A
    (3)   2 UO
    (4) Cb

*(b) (1) ~De   A
    (2) Fe   A
    (3)   PA
    (4)   3 UO
    (5)   4,2 →O
    (6) De & ~De
    (7) ~(x)(Fx → Dx)

Instructions for exercises 5 through 9: Symbolize each argument (on one horizontal line) using the suggested abbreviations, and establish its validity by constructing a formal proof.

5. The clerk in this "Eb and Flo" comic strip reasons:

   CROOKS don't BUY peat moss. Flo is purchasing peat moss. So, Flo is not a crook.

May 19, 1973. © 1973 United Feature Syndicate, Inc.

6. Physiologist Knut Schmidt-Nielsen writes in *Scientific American:*

   All birds have . . . pneumatized [hollow] bones. (Even the ostrich has the larger leg bones filled with air. . . . Pneumatized bones are therefore not restricted to birds that can fly.)[7]

   His argument:

[7] "How Birds Breathe," *Scientific American* (December, 1971), p. 73.

The <u>ostrich</u> is a species having pneumatized BONES. The ostrich is not a species of FLYERS. Therefore, it is not the case that every species with pneumatized bones is a flying species.

7. When Disney World was under construction in central Florida, Miami Beach hoteliers debated the effect this attraction would have on tourism in south Florida. A newspaper feature examined the reasoning on both sides, and summarized one argument as follows:

> . . . *Anything that BRINGS new people and more people to Florida must HELP Miami Beach; <u>Disney</u> World is going to promote Florida and bring millions of first-time <u>visitors</u> to the state; ergo, Disney World must help, not harm, Miami Beach.*[8]

($Bx = x$ brings more people to Florida, $Hx = x$ helps Miami Beach, $d = $ Disney World)

8. Otto argues:

The <u>woman</u> on the blanket is ALLOWED on the beach. She is a DOG. So, the claim that no dogs are allowed on the beach is mistaken.

The strip equivocates on the term 'dog'.

August 31, 1973, © King Features Syndicate.

*9. A news story about the 1972 Democratic National Convention includes this paragraph:

> As KEYNOTE speaker, <u>Askew</u> cannot be a delegate under any circumstances. Askew's aides said the keynote speaker cannot be pledged to any candidate, and all Florida DELEGATES will be PLEDGED.[9]

This passage is an argument with the conclusion that Governor Askew will not be a delegate (from Florida). The argument has three premises. ($Kx = x$ is a keynote speaker, $a = $ Askew, $Dx = x$ is a Florida delegate, $Px = x$ is pledged to some candidate)

---

[8] "Disney World Cheers Hotel Men" (New York Times News Service), *Miami News*, April 5, 1971, p. 12-A.

[9] Louis Salome, "Delegate Dilemma if Wallace Wins," *Miami News*, March 1, 1972, p. 15-A.

3.2
Existential Quantifier Out

This question and its answer appeared in a Hy Gardner column:

> Q: *I would like to work as a Playboy bunny. But now I hear that to get the job you must be a virgin. Is this so?*
>
> D. McSarren, Oklahoma City

> A: *In the early days of the Playboy Club in Chicago, one of Hugh Hefner's den mothers insisted this was a rigid rule. If it was (which I doubt) it ceased to be when married bunnies were permitted to join Hef's hutch.*[10]

Gardner advances this argument:

> Some BUNNIES are MARRIED. Consequently, since no one married is a VIRGIN, the claim that only virgins are bunnies is false.

The argument symbolized:

$$(\exists x)(Bx \,\&\, Mx), (x)(Mx \rightarrow \sim Vx) \vdash \sim(x)(Bx \rightarrow Vx)$$

It is evident that in order to complete a proof for this valid argument we must have a rule which allows us to eliminate the existential quantifier in the symbolized first premise.

> **The Existential Quantifier Out Rule (EO): From an existential quantification derive any instance of it, *provided that* the name being introduced does not occur in the symbolization of the argument being tested or on any line above the line derived.**

We define an *existential quantification* as a wff beginning with an existential quantifier. An *instance* of an existential quantification is a wff which results from deleting the quantifier and replacing each of the remaining occurrences of the variable by the same name.[11] The EO Rule incorporates two restrictions (see the clause following 'provided that'). The need for these restrictions will be explained later in this section.

---

[10] From *Glad You Asked That*, by Marilyn Gardner and Hy Gardner, courtesy of Field Newspaper Syndicate.

[11] These definitions will require modification later.

We can now construct a proof for the "bunny" argument:

(1) $(\exists x)(Bx \, \& \, Mx)$ A
(2) $(x)(Mx \rightarrow \sim Vx)$ A
(3) $(x)(Bx \rightarrow Vx)$ PA
(4) $Ba \, \& \, Ma$ 1 EO
(5) $Ma \rightarrow \sim Va$ 2 UO
(6) $Ba \rightarrow Va$ 3 UO
(7) Ma 4 &O
(8) $\sim Va$ 5,7 $\rightarrow$O
(9) Ba 4 &O
(10) Va 6,9 $\rightarrow$O
(11) $Va \, \& \sim Va$ 10,8 &I
(12) $\sim(x)(Bx \rightarrow Vx)$ 3–11 $\sim$I

Line 4 is an instance of the existential quantification on line 1. Furthermore, the name introduced on line 4 (*a*) does not occur in the symbolization of the argument, nor does it occur on lines 1 through 3. Thus the EO Rule was correctly applied. The name to which I instantiated on the fourth line was selected at random; any other name would have served as well. However, having chosen *a* for line 4, I had to instantiate to it again on lines 5 and 6 in order to complete the proof. The purpose of the EO Rule is to permit us to derive from existential quantifications wffs to which the propositional inference rules apply. Consider the above proof. The Ampersand Out Rule cannot be applied to line 1, because that wff is not a conjunction (its main symbol is not an ampersand), but the rule *can* be applied to line 4 (which was derived from line 1 by the EO Rule).

I will construct a second proof employing the EO Rule. The following argument summarizes part of the Supreme Court's thinking in its ruling on the case of *Brown* v. *the Board of Education of Topeka* (1954):

> Any school system with SEPARATE facilities for its white and black children generates INFERIORITY feelings among the black students. No system which creates such feelings in its black children has EQUAL facilities. So, it is not the case that there are school systems with separate but equal facilities.

($Sx = x$ is a school system with separate facilities, $Ix = x$ is a school system which generates inferiority feelings among black students, $Ex = x$ is a school system with equal facilities) The argument may be symbolized:

$(x)(Sx \rightarrow Ix), (x)(Ix \rightarrow \sim Ex) \vdash \sim(\exists x)(Sx \, \& \, Ex)$

A proof:

(1)	$(x)(Sx \rightarrow Ix)$	A
(2)	$(x)(Ix \rightarrow \sim Ex)$	A
(3)	$(\exists x)(Sx \ \& \ Ex)$	PA
(4)	$Sb \ \& \ Eb$	3 EO
(5)	$Sb \rightarrow Ib$	1 UO
(6)	$Ib \rightarrow \sim Eb$	2 UO
(7)	Sb	4 &O
(8)	Ib	5,7 $\rightarrow$O
(9)	$\sim Eb$	6,8 $\rightarrow$O
(10)	Eb	4 &O
(11)	$Eb \ \& \sim Eb$	10,9 &I
(12)	$\sim(\exists x)(Sx \ \& \ Ex)$	3–11 $\sim$I

Notice that the existential quantification on line 3 was instantiated before the universal quantifications on lines 1 and 2. This was done to ensure satisfaction of the second restriction on the EO Rule—the requirement that the name introduced not appear on any higher line. This procedural principle should be followed:

Wherever possible, employ the EO Rule before using the UO Rule.

I will conclude the section by considering two questions: *Why is the EO Rule sound?* and *Why are the two restrictions needed?* Consider the statement 'Some RABBIS are JAPANESE' and the existential quantification, F1, which symbolizes it.

(F1) $(\exists x)(Rx \ \& \ Jx)$

The EO Rule permits us to derive F2, an instance of F1 (where c satisfies the two restrictions on the rule).

(F2) $Rc \ \& \ Jc$

Is it legitimate to infer F2 from F1? A justification can be formulated as an argument:

F1 is true iff (if and only if) there is at least one individual to whom the predicates R and J can be correctly ascribed. If there is at least one such individual, "c" will serve as a name of that individual (or one of those individuals). If there is some individual to whom R and J can be correctly ascribed and "c" names that individual, then F2 is true. It follows that if F1 is true, F2 is true.

This propositional argument can be symbolized:

$$D \leftrightarrow A, A \rightarrow C, (A \,\&\, C) \rightarrow E \vdash D \rightarrow E$$

Is it valid? This justification of the EO Rule presupposes that the name employed in the instance has only this connotation—that it is the name being arbitrarily assigned to some individual in virtue of which F1 is true (if it is true). The purpose of the two restrictions on the EO Rule is to guarantee the arbitrary selection of the name.

The best way to demonstrate the need for the restrictions is to show that without them it would be possible to construct "proofs" for invalid arguments. Here is an obviously invalid argument:

Some DEMOCRATS tend BARS. Thus, Bill Buckley is a Democrat.

The argument is symbolized:

$$(\exists x)(Dx \,\&\, Bx) \vdash Db$$

A "proof":

(1)	$(\exists x)(Dx \,\&\, Bx)$	A
(2)	Db & Bb	1 EO (ERROR!)
(3)	Db	2 &O

The move to line 2 violates the first restriction on the EO Rule, since the name introduced appears in the symbolization of the argument. In symbolizing the argument I chose b to refer to Bill Buckley. Thus, when I instantiated on line 2, b was not a randomly selected name.

A second obviously fallacious argument:

Some Democrats do not tend bars. So, it is false that some Democrats do tend bars.

That this argument is invalid follows from the fact that its premise is true while its conclusion is false. The conclusion denies the true assertion that some Democrats tend bars. The argument is symbolized:

$$(\exists x)(Dx \,\&\, {\sim}Bx) \vdash {\sim}(\exists x)(Dx \,\&\, Bx)$$

A "proof":

(1)	$(\exists x)(Dx \,\&\, {\sim}Bx)$	A
(2)	$(\exists x)(Dx \,\&\, Bx)$	PA
(3)	De & ~Be	1 EO

(4)	De & Be	2 EO (ERROR!)
(5)	Be	4 &O
(6)	~Be	3 &O
(7)	Be & ~Be	5,6 &I
(8)	~(∃x)(Dx & Bx)	2-7 ~I

The derivation of line 4 violates the second restriction on the EO Rule, since the name used on line 4 occurs on a preceding line (3). As *e* was already assigned a use on line 3 (to name some individual that makes line 1 a truth), it was not randomly selected on line 4. These two "bartender" arguments show the necessity for the two restrictions on the rule. Fortunately, no other restrictions are needed. The EO Rule is our only restricted predicate inference rule.

EXERCISES

10. Complete the following proofs. Every assumption has been identified.

*(a)
(1)	(∃x)(Cx & Nx)	A
(2)	(x)(Cx → ~Nx)	PA
(3)	Ca & Na	1 EO
(4)		2 UO
(5)	Ca	
(6)		4,5 →O
(7)		3 &O
(8)		7,6 &I
(9)	~(x)(Cx → ~Nx)	2-8 ~I

(b)
(1)	(x)(Dx → Ex)	A
(2)	(∃x)(Fx & ~Ex)	A
(3)		PA
(4)	Fg & ~Eg	
(5)		1 UO
(6)		3 UO
(7)	Fg	
(8)		6,7 →O
(9)	Eg	
(10)		4 &O

(11)   9,10 &I

(12)   ~(x)(Fx → Dx)

Instructions for exercises 11 through 14: Symbolize the arguments and construct proofs for them.

11. One of my students wrote on an exam:

> *Soft, or moderate, determinism states that every event is caused and some events are not caused.*

(The position outlined is not that of soft determinism.[12]) Demonstrate the inconsistency of the view described by the student by proving that 'Every EVENT is CAUSED' entails[13] the negation of 'Some events are not caused'.

*12. The philosopher C. D. Broad attacked the view that mental events are physical events. In *The Mind and Its Place in Nature*, he wrote:

> *About a molecular movement it is perfectly reasonable to raise the question "Is it swift or slow, straight or circular and so on?" About the awareness of a red patch it is nonsensical to ask whether it is a swift or slow awareness, a straight or circular awareness, and so on.[14]*

We may paraphrase Broad's reasoning in this way:

It makes sense to say of any molecular MOVEMENT that it is STRAIGHT. It does not make sense to say of any AWARENESS of a red patch that it is straight. Hence, it is false that awarenesses of a red patch are sometimes molecular movements.

($Mx = x$ is a molecular movement, $Sx = x$ is something of which it makes sense to say that it is straight, $Ax = x$ is an awareness of a red patch)

13. News story:

> *RIO DE JANEIRO — Prostitutes from Rio's red-light district did so well in an adult literacy course that one of them got a job as a real estate agent, police said today.*
>
> *Police Chief Armando Pereira handed out literacy diplomas to 24 of the prostitutes and declared, "This disproves the theory that only half-wits exist in this profession."[15]*

The chief's inference:

Some PROSTITUTES are LITERATE. HALF-WITS aren't literate. Thus, the theory that only half-wits exist in this profession is false.

[12]*Soft determinism* is the view that although every event is caused, some human acts are free.

[13]One statement *entails* a second iff the argument which has the first statement as sole premise and the second statement as conclusion is valid.

[14](London: Routledge & Kegan Paul, 1925), p. 623.

[15]"Prostitutes Given Literacy Diplomas," *Miami News*, January 11, 1971, p. 3-A.

14. On an exam in Introduction to Philosophy I asked:

> *How would the hard determinist answer the question, "Could a machine have free will?"*

One student answered (in part):

> *The hard determinist says that all events are caused. Therefore all machine actions (which are also events) are caused. Therefore a machine could not have free will.*

Formalizing this a bit more we reach:

All EVENTS are CAUSED. All MACHINE actions are events. Nothing caused is FREE. Therefore, it is false that there are free machine actions.

202. (CHALLENGING) Construct a seven-line proof for exercise 11.

chapter four

More Proofs

4.1
Quantifier Exchange

In September, 1971 the inmates of Attica State Prison staged a revolt. After an assault by police and National Guardsmen ended the revolt it was discovered that nine hostages had been slain. It was not immediately clear who had killed the hostages. Conflicting reports were made, each backed up by an argument. On one view, all of the dead hostages were killed (accidentally) by the attacking police.[1]

> [According to autopsy reports] every dead HOSTAGE died of GUN-SHOT wounds. None who died of such wounds was killed by INMATES [as the inmates had no guns]. Therefore, none of the dead hostages was killed by inmates.

Ignoring the bracketed material, I symbolize the argument:

$(x)(Hx \rightarrow Gx), (x)(Gx \rightarrow \sim Ix) \vdash (x)(Hx \rightarrow \sim Ix)$

---

[1] "Guns Killed 9 Hostages at Jail, Autopsies Show," *Miami News*, September 14, 1971, p. 1-A.

($Hx = x$ is a dead hostage, $Gx = x$ dies of gunshot wounds, $Ix = x$ is killed by inmates) On the other hand, prison officials claimed that at least some of the hostages were killed by prisoners.[2] Their argument:

> [According to autopsy reports] some of the dead hostages were killed BEFORE the assault took place. Anyone slain before the assault was killed by prisoners. So, some of the dead hostages were killed by inmates.

Symbolization:

$(\exists x)(Hx \ \& \ Bx), (x)(Bx \rightarrow Ix) \vdash (\exists x)(Hx \ \& \ Ix)$

These two valid arguments have contradictory conclusions. It follows that at least one of them has a false premise.[3]

The two "Attica" arguments are *categorical syllogisms*. A categorical syllogism is an argument with these features:

(1) It consists of three statements.

(2) Each statement is an *A*, *E*, *I*, or *O* statement.

(3) It involves three predicates, each occurring in two statements.

There are 256 forms of categorical syllogisms. Most contemporary logicians assess 15 of these forms as valid and the remaining 241 as invalid. For practical purposes, the 15 valid syllogism-forms can be reduced to the six forms listed in this table:

Six Valid Syllogism-Forms

All $\mathcal{D}$ are $\mathcal{E}$	No $\mathcal{D}$ are $\mathcal{E}$
All $\mathcal{F}$ are $\mathcal{D}$	All $\mathcal{F}$ are $\mathcal{D}$
So all $\mathcal{F}$ are $\mathcal{E}$	So no $\mathcal{F}$ are $\mathcal{E}$
All $\mathcal{D}$ are $\mathcal{E}$	No $\mathcal{D}$ are $\mathcal{E}$
Some $\mathcal{F}$ are $\mathcal{D}$	Some $\mathcal{F}$ are $\mathcal{D}$
So some $\mathcal{F}$ are $\mathcal{E}$	So some $\mathcal{F}$ are not $\mathcal{E}$
Some $\mathcal{D}$ are not $\mathcal{E}$	All $\mathcal{E}$ are $\mathcal{D}$
All $\mathcal{D}$ are $\mathcal{F}$	Some $\mathcal{F}$ are not $\mathcal{D}$
So some $\mathcal{F}$ are not $\mathcal{E}$	So some $\mathcal{F}$ are not $\mathcal{E}$

Arguments exhibiting essentially these six forms will be found in the exercise set at the end of the chapter. The study of categorical syllogisms,

---

[2] "2 Slain Before Assault Started, Autopsies Show," *Miami News*, September 14, 1971, p. 5-C.

[3] My reasoning: At least one of the arguments has a false conclusion. Both arguments are valid. Any valid argument with a false conclusion has a false premise. Therefore, at least one of the arguments has a false premise. (Does this argument belong to predicate logic? Is it valid?)

called *syllogistic logic* or *Aristotelian logic*, dominated formal logic from the fourth century B.C. through the last century.[4] Predicate logic, developed largely in the present century, includes within its scope all categorical syllogisms plus many arguments which syllogistic logic is unable to treat.

Let's return to the first of the "Attica" syllogisms and attempt to construct a formal proof for it.

$$(x)(Hx \rightarrow Gx), (x)(Gx \rightarrow \sim Ix) \vdash (x)(Hx \rightarrow \sim Ix)$$

As the conclusion of this argument contains a quantifier and we have no "In" rules for quantifiers, it is clear that the proof will employ the Tilde Out strategy. Accordingly, I make a provisional assumption of the negation of the argument's conclusion. The proof begins:

(1) $(x)(Hx \rightarrow Gx)$ A

(2) $(x)(Gx \rightarrow \sim Ix)$ A

(3) $\sim(x)(Hx \rightarrow \sim Ix)$ PA

The wff on line 3 is not a universal quantification, and therefore the UO Rule cannot be applied to it. A few of the propositional inference rules can be applied to line 3, but their use will not advance the proof; the path is blocked. This problem (or one similar to it) will occur in the proof of *any* syllogism. It is obvious that we require an additional rule of inference.

The Quantifier Exchange Rule (QE): From the negation of a universal quantification derive the wff which results from replacing the quantifier by an existential quantifier and transposing the tilde and the quantifier. From the negation of an existential quantification derive the wff which results from replacing the quantifier by a universal quantifier and transposing the tilde and the quantifier.

The rule can be phrased more simply with the aid of script symbols:[5]

From $\sim(x)\mathcal{A}x$ derive $(\exists x)\sim\mathcal{A}x$.

From $\sim(\exists x)\mathcal{A}x$ derive $(x)\sim\mathcal{A}x$.

---

[4] For a fuller account of syllogistic logic see Chapter Two of Stephen F. Barker, *The Elements of Logic* (2d ed.; New York: McGraw-Hill Book Company, 1974).

[5] '$\sim(x)\mathcal{A}x$' represents the negation of any universal quantification and '$(\exists x)\sim\mathcal{A}x$' represents the wff which results from replacing the quantifier by an existential quantifier and transposing the tilde and the quantifier. '$\sim(\exists x)\mathcal{A}x$' represents the negation of any existential quantification and '$(x)\sim\mathcal{A}x$' represents the wff which results from replacing the quantifier by a universal quantifier and transposing the tilde and the quantifier.

With the aid of the QE Rule the proof for the first "Attica" syllogism is easily completed:

(1)	$(x)(Hx \rightarrow Gx)$	A
(2)	$(x)(Gx \rightarrow \sim Ix)$	A
(3)	$\sim(x)(Hx \rightarrow \sim Ix)$	PA
(4)	$(\exists x)\sim(Hx \rightarrow \sim Ix)$	3 QE
(5)	$\sim(Ha \rightarrow \sim Ia)$	4 EO
(6)	$Ha \rightarrow Ga$	1 UO
(7)	$Ga \rightarrow \sim Ia$	2 UO
(8)	$Ha \rightarrow \sim Ia$	6,7 CH
(9)	$(Ha \rightarrow \sim Ia) \,\&\, \sim(Ha \rightarrow \sim Ia)$	8,5 &I
(10)	$(x)(Hx \rightarrow \sim Ix)$	3–9 $\sim$O

The purpose of the QE Rule is to transform *the negation of a quantification* into *a quantification* so that the UO or EO Rule may be used. Neither the UO nor the EO Rule applies to line 3 of this proof, but EO applies to line 4.

The second "Attica" syllogism provides another example of the use of the QE Rule. This argument was symbolized:

$$(\exists x)(Hx \,\&\, Bx), \ (x)(Bx \rightarrow Ix) \vdash (\exists x)(Hx \,\&\, Ix)$$

Proofs for *all* syllogisms (and for many other arguments) can be analyzed into seven stages. To illustrate this I divide the following proof into these stages.

STAGES

i	(1)	$(\exists x)(Hx \,\&\, Bx)$	A
	(2)	$(x)(Bx \rightarrow Ix)$	A
ii	(3)	$\sim(\exists x)(Hx \,\&\, Ix)$	PA
iii	(4)	$(x)\sim(Hx \,\&\, Ix)$	3 QE
iv	(5)	$Ha \,\&\, Ba$	1 EO
v	(6)	$Ba \rightarrow Ia$	2 UO
	(7)	$\sim(Ha \,\&\, Ia)$	4 UO
vi	(8)	Ba	5 &O
	(9)	Ia	6,8 $\rightarrow$O
	(10)	$\sim Ha$	7,9 CA
	(11)	Ha	5 &O
	(12)	$Ha \,\&\, \sim Ha$	11,10 &I
vii	(13)	$(\exists x)(Hx \,\&\, Ix)$	3–12 $\sim$O

The seven stages:

> (i) The premises of the argument are assumed.
>
> (ii) A provisional assumption is made of the negation of the conclusion (in anticipation of stage seven).
>
> (iii) The QE Rule is applied to assumptions which are negations of quantifications.
>
> (iv) The EO Rule is applied to existential quantifications.
>
> (v) The UO Rule is applied to universal quantifications.
>
> (vi) A standard contradiction is derived (by propositional inference rules) from the wffs reached in stages four and five.
>
> (vii) The conclusion is obtained by Tilde Out.

We can justify the QE Rule by noting the intuitive soundness of English versions of the rule. An English counterpart of the first form of the rule:

> From 'It is false that everything is $\mathcal{Q}$' derive 'Something is not $\mathcal{Q}$'.

By substituting a specific predicate for the script '$\mathcal{Q}$' and employing more colloquial English we reach a version of the rule which is even more obviously correct:

> From 'Not all things are physical' derive 'Some things aren't physical'.

Two English counterparts of the second form of the rule — one abstract and the other concrete:

> From 'It is false that there is an $\mathcal{Q}$' derive 'Each thing is not $\mathcal{Q}$'.
>
> From 'It's false that ghosts exist' derive 'Nothing is a ghost'.

With the UO, EO, and QE Rules at our disposal, we are in a position to explore some logical features of A, E, I, and O statements. A and O statements which have the same predicates (in the same order) are *contradictories*. Two statements are contradictories iff it is logically necessary that one be true and the other false. S1 and S2 are contradictories.

> (S1) All EVENTS are CAUSED.
>
> (S2) Some events are not caused.

These two statements cannot both be true, nor can they both be false. The following principle connects the relation of "contradiction" with the relation of "logical equivalence":

Two statements are contradictories iff the first statement is logically equivalent to the negation of the second.

We can prove that S1 and S2 are contradictories by demonstrating that S1 and the negation of S2 entail each other. Exercise 11 (Chapter Three) concerned S1's entailing the negation of S2. I show now that the negation of S2 entails S1:

(1)	$\sim(\exists x)(Ex \,\&\, \sim Cx)$	A
(2)	$\sim(x)(Ex \rightarrow Cx)$	PA
(3)	$(x)\sim(Ex \,\&\, \sim Cx)$	1 QE
(4)	$(\exists x)\sim(Ex \rightarrow Cx)$	2 QE
(5)	$\sim(Ea \rightarrow Ca)$	4 EO
(6)	$\sim(Ea \,\&\, \sim Ca)$	3 UO
(7)	$Ea \rightarrow Ca$	6 AR
(8)	$(Ea \rightarrow Ca) \,\&\, \sim(Ea \rightarrow Ca)$	7,5 &I
(9)	$(x)(Ex \rightarrow Cx)$	2-8 $\sim$O

I and *E* statements with the same predicates are also contradictories. S3 and S4 serve as examples:

(S3) Some conservatives are nudists.

(S4) No conservatives are nudists.

These statements are contradictories iff S3 and the negation of S4 are logically equivalent. Exercise 10(a) in Chapter Three treated S3's entailment of the negation of S4. When you work exercise 21 at the end of this chapter you will prove that the negation of S4 entails S3.

The *converse* of an *A*, *E*, *I*, or *O* statement is the statement which results when you switch the predicates. For example, S6 is the converse of S5.

(S5) Some RABBIS are JAPANESE.

(S6) Some Japanese are rabbis.

An *I* statement and its converse are logically equivalent. (In logicians' terminology, an *I* statement is validly *convertible*.) This proof demonstrates that S5 entails S6.

(1)	$(\exists x)(Rx \,\&\, Jx)$	A
(2)	$\sim(\exists x)(Jx \,\&\, Rx)$	PA
(3)	$(x)\sim(Jx \,\&\, Rx)$	2 QE
(4)	$Ra \,\&\, Ja$	1 EO

(5)	~(Ja & Ra)	3 UO
(6)	Ra	4 &O
(7)	~Ja	5,6 CA
(8)	Ja	4 &O
(9)	Ja & ~Ja	8,7 &I
(10)	(∃x)(Jx & Rx)	2–9 ~O

A formally identical proof establishes that S6 entails S5. *E* statements are also validly convertible. S4 and S7 are logically equivalent.

(S4)   No conservatives are nudists.

(S7)   No nudists are conservatives.

Exercise 17 at the end of the chapter concerns the convertibility of *E* statements.

Neither *A* nor *O* statements can be converted validly. It should be clear that S8 and S9 have different content, and that S10 and S11 are non-equivalent.

(S8)   All "uppers" are drugs.

(S9)   All drugs are "uppers."

(S10)   Some reptiles are not snakes.

(S11)   Some snakes are not reptiles.

S8 and S9 (S10 and S11) have different truth values; hence, they cannot be logically equivalent. This result will be reached more formally in exercise 43 (Chapter Six).

Earlier in the chapter I claimed that the 15 syllogism-forms regarded as valid by most contemporary logicians can be *reduced* to six forms. This reduction is achieved simply by converting *E* and *I* statement-forms and (in some cases) switching the premises. By this method, for example, we can reduce argument-form one to argument-form two:

(1)   No $\mathcal{E}$ are $\mathcal{D}$, Some $\mathcal{D}$ are $\mathcal{F}$, So some $\mathcal{F}$ are not $\mathcal{E}$

(2)   No $\mathcal{D}$ are $\mathcal{E}$, Some $\mathcal{F}$ are $\mathcal{D}$, So some $\mathcal{F}$ are not $\mathcal{E}$

An argument which is like a syllogism except that it has more than two premises is called a *sorites*.[6] One of my colleagues employed a sorites when he was a child to reach a startling conclusion:

---

[6] More precisely, a sorites is an argument having these features: (1) It consists of four or more statements. (2) Each statement is an *A, E, I,* or *O* statement. (3) The number of predicates equals the number of statements. (4) Each predicate occurs in two statements. (The term 'sorites' is pronounced "SUH-RIGHT'-EASE." Plural: 'sorites'.)

Whoever engages in INTERCOURSE is EVIL.

MINISTERS are not evil.

Some ministers have CHILDREN.

Therefore, some who have children have never had intercourse.

The argument contains statements exhibiting the four basic general forms. It is symbolized:

$$(x)(Ix \rightarrow Ex), (x)(Mx \rightarrow \sim Ex), (\exists x)(Mx \& Cx) \vdash (\exists x)(Cx \& \sim Ix)$$

A proof of validity for this sorites will be somewhat longer than, but in other respects similar to, a syllogistic proof:

(1)	$(x)(Ix \rightarrow Ex)$	A
(2)	$(x)(Mx \rightarrow \sim Ex)$	A
(3)	$(\exists x)(Mx \& Cx)$	A
(4)	$\sim (\exists x)(Cx \& \sim Ix)$	PA
(5)	$(x)\sim(Cx \& \sim Ix)$	4 QE
(6)	Ma & Ca	3 EO
(7)	Ia $\rightarrow$ Ea	1 UO
(8)	Ma $\rightarrow \sim$Ea	2 UO
(9)	$\sim(Ca \& \sim Ia)$	5 UO
(10)	Ma	6 &O
(11)	$\sim$Ea	8,10 $\rightarrow$O
(12)	$\sim$Ia	7,11 MT
(13)	$\sim$Ca	9,12 CA
(14)	Ca	6 &O
(15)	Ca & $\sim$Ca	14,13 &I
(16)	$(\exists x)(Cx \& \sim Ix)$	4–15 $\sim$O

Exercise 25 at the end of the chapter concerns a sorites with four premises.

In this chapter and the preceding one, three predicate inference rules have been presented. These rules, when added to the group of eighteen propositional inference rules listed on pages 203 and 204, form a set which is sufficient for constructing a formal proof for *any* valid symbolized argument that is formulated in the notation presented in this book. In logicians' terminology, the set of rules is *complete*. The set is also *consistent;* that is, no proof can be constructed with these rules for an invalid symbolized argument.[7]

---

[7] For a discussion of the completeness and consistency of predicate logic see Part Three of Geoffrey Hunter, *Metalogic* (Berkeley and Los Angeles: University of California Press, 1971).

EXERCISES

15. Complete the following proofs. Every assumption has been identified. Note that (b) and (c) are alternative proofs for one argument.

*(a)   (1)   ~(x)(Ax → Bx)   A
      (2)   ~(∃x)(Ax & ~Bx)   PA
      (3)   1 QE
      (4)   2 QE
      (5)   ~(Af → Bf)
      (6)   4 UO
      (7)   Af → Bf
      (8)   7,5 &I
      (9)   (∃x)(Ax & ~Bx)   2–8 ~O

(b)   (1)   (x)(Cx → ~Dx)   A
      (2)   (x)(Ex → Dx)   A
      (3)   ~(x)(Cx → ~Ex)   PA
      (4)   3 QE
      (5)   ~(Cg → ~Eg)
      (6)   1 UO
      (7)   2 UO
      (8)   Cg & ~~Eg
      (9)   Cg
     (10)   6,9 →O
     (11)   7,10 MT
     (12)   8 &O
     (13)   ~Eg & ~~Eg
     (14)   (x)(Cx → ~Ex)   3–13 ~O

(c)   (1)   (x)(Cx → ~Dx)   A
      (2)   (x)(Ex → Dx)   A
      (3)   PA
      (4)   (∃x)~(Cx → ~Ex)
      (5)   4 EO
      (6)   Ch → ~Dh
      (7)   Eh → Dh
      (8)   7 CN
      (9)   6,8 CH
     (10)   9,5 &I
     (11)   (x)(Cx → ~Ex)   3–10 ~O

Instructions for exercises 16 through 25: Symbolize the arguments and construct proofs for them.

*16. Sign in a supermarket:

> *SHOPLIFTING IS STEALING*
> *STEALING IS A SERIOUS CRIME*

This is an argument with an unstated conclusion. We can formulate it as follows:

Any case of shoplifting is a case of stealing. All cases of stealing are serious crimes. Hence, all instances of shoplifting are serious crimes.

($Ax = x$ is a case of shoplifting, $Bx = x$ is a case of stealing, $Cx = x$ is a serious crime)

17. I John 4:18 includes the following sentences:

> (S1)   ". . . Perfect love casts out fear."
> (S2)   ". . . He who fears is not perfected in love."[8]

Prove that S1 entails S2. This is an instance of the convertibility of *E* statements. S1 may be paraphrased as "He who has perfect LOVE has no FEAR."

18. Bertrand Russell writes in *A History of Western Philosophy:*

> *The syllogism is only one kind of deductive argument. In mathematics, which is wholly deductive, syllogisms hardly ever occur.*[9]

Syllogisms are uncommon in mathematics but common in philosophy — this passage being a case in point. Russell's syllogism:

MATHEMATICAL arguments are all DEDUCTIVE. Many mathematical arguments are not SYLLOGISMS. So, some deductive arguments are not syllogisms.

*19. When James MacArthur (of "Hawaii Five-O") dropped out of college, he offered this justification for his action:

> *Some of the most educated people have never been to college. My mother [Helen Hayes] never went past high school — and she holds eleven honorary degrees.*[10]

MacArthur makes the doubtful assumption that there is a connection between holding honorary degrees and being educated. Setting that aside we discern this argument:

Helen Hayes did not go to COLLEGE. She is an EDUCATED person. It follows that some educated people did not attend college.

20. In the Sixth *Meditation*, Descartes writes:

> *I first take notice here that there is a great difference between the mind*

---

[8] The Bible, Revised Standard Version (New York: Thomas Nelson & Sons, 1952).
[9] (New York: Simon and Schuster, 1945), p. 198.
[10] Hy Gardner, "Ask Hy Gardner," *Miami News*, September 7, 1971, p. 8-B.

and the body, in that the body, from its nature, is always divisible and the mind is completely indivisible.[11]

He is reasoning syllogistically:

BODIES are always DIVISIBLE. MINDS are indivisible. Thus, no minds are bodies.

21. *I* and *E* statements with the same predicates (for example, S3 and S4) are contradictories.

(S3)   Some CONSERVATIVES are NUDISTS.

(S4)   No conservatives are nudists.

Exercise 10(a) in Chapter Three is a proof that S3 entails the negation of S4. Show that the negation of S4 also entails S3 (thereby completing the demonstration that S3 and S4 are contradictories).

22. A television news story concerned an Englishman who invested in stocks in his dog's name when he learned that British law prohibits collecting taxes from (nonhuman) animals. The legal loophole he discovered is the subject of this syllogism:

Some ANIMALS own PROPERTY. Therefore, since animals can't be TAXED, some property owners are not subject to taxation.

23. *Newsweek* correspondent Kevin P. Buckley claimed in a report filed in 1972 that during a 1968 "pacification" campaign in South Vietnam's Mekong Delta, U.S. firepower killed as many as 5,000 noncombatant civilians. One of his arguments was based on the fact that while 10,899 "enemy" were killed, only 748 weapons were captured. Buckley wrote:

There is overwhelming evidence that virtually all the Viet Cong were well armed. Simple civilians were, of course, not armed. And the enormous discrepancy between the body count and the number of captured weapons is hard to explain—except by the conclusion that many victims were unarmed, innocent civilians.[12]

This syllogism paraphrases Buckley's argument:

All the Viet CONG were ARMED. Some of those KILLED were not armed. This proves that some who were killed were not Viet Cong.

24. After a medical checkup including X-rays, I had this conversation with my doctor:

DOCTOR: *There is a polyp on your large intestine.*
HOWARD: *What is the difference between a polyp and a tumor?*
DOCTOR: *All polyps are tumors, but not all tumors are polyps. Polyps are . . .*

---

[11] Rene Descartes, *Meditations on First Philosophy*, tr. by Laurence J. Lafleur (Indianapolis, Ind.: The Bobbs-Merrill Company, Inc., 1951, 1960), p. 81.

[12] "Pacification's Deadly Price," *Newsweek*, June 19, 1972, p. 43. Copyright 1972 by Newsweek, Inc. All rights reserved. Reprinted by permission.

In short order I drew the following chilling inference:

There is a POLYP on my LARGE intestine. All polyps are TUMORS. So, there is a tumor on my large intestine.

Happily, further tests showed the first premise and the conclusion of this syllogism to be false. ($Lx = x$ is on my large intestine)

25. This bit of Shakespearean wit is a sorites:

Clown. . . . *He that comforts my wife is the cherisher of my flesh and blood; he that cherishes my flesh and blood loves my flesh and blood; he that loves my flesh and blood is my friend: ergo, he that kisses my wife is my friend.*[13]

Add this unstated premise:

He that kisses my wife comforts my wife.

($Ax = x$ comforts my wife, $Bx = x$ cherishes my flesh and blood, $Lx = x$ loves my flesh and blood, $Fx = x$ is my friend, $Kx = x$ kisses my wife)

203. (CHALLENGING) Construct a ten-line proof for exercise 21. (Note: any nine-line "proof" is mistaken.)

---

[13]*All's Well that Ends Well,* act I, scene iii, lines 45–49 (Cambridge: Cambridge University Press, 1929, 1968), p. 14.

chapter five

Nonstandard Problems

5.1
Symbolization

In Chapter Two we discussed the symbolization of singular statements and statements of the A, E, I, and O types. We may refer to such statements as *standard statements*. Chapters Three and Four treated arguments composed of standard statements (and their negations). Many statements which can be analyzed in predicate logic are not standard statements. The present section is devoted to the symbolization of these nonstandard statements, and section 5.2 deals with arguments containing such statements.

Let's begin with general statements containing only one predicate.

Something is MATERIAL.	$(\exists x)Mx$
Everything is material.	$(x)Mx$
Something isn't material.	$(\exists x)\sim Mx$
Nothing is material	$(x)\sim Mx$

No two of these four wffs are logically equivalent, but for each wff there is a logically equivalent formula which involves the other quantifier. The wffs on each line of this table are equivalent:

(∃x)Mx	~(x)~Mx
(x)Mx	~(∃x)~Mx
(∃x)~Mx	~(x)Mx
(x)~Mx	~(∃x)Mx

This table suggests (what is true) that any sentence symbolizable by a wff containing an existential quantifier can also be symbolized by some wff involving a universal quantifier (and vice versa).

Many statements that contain *two* predicates are not of the A, E, I, or O varieties. Some examples:

Some things are either TASTY or FATTENING.	(∃x)(Tx ∨ Fx)
Some things are neither tasty nor fattening.	(∃x)~(Tx ∨ Fx)
Each thing is either tasty or fattening.	(x)(Tx ∨ Fx)
Everything is both tasty and fattening.	(x)(Tx & Fx)
A thing is tasty iff it is fattening.	(x)(Tx ↔ Fx)
This <u>drumstick</u> is fattening but not tasty.	Fd & ~Td

Definitions often are symbolized as universally quantified biconditionals. Definition S1, for example, is symbolized by F1.

(S1) "Heavy SPAR: BARITE." (Webster)

(F1) (x)(Sx ↔ Bx)

(F2) (x)(Sx → Bx)

F2 is inadequate as a symbolization of S1. S1 and F1 claim that each piece of heavy spar is barite *and* vice versa, while F2 makes only the first of these claims. I should add that you cannot always tell whether a statement is a definition by scrutinizing it in isolation; you may need to examine its context.

Some statements differ from A, E, I, and O statements principally in containing three (rather than two) predicates. The following sentences resemble A statements:

SENTENCE	SYMBOLIZATION	SOURCE
"All BIRDS have two LEGS and two WINGS."	(x) [Bx → (Lx & Wx)]	*Scientific American*
"All of my FRIENDS who are BOYS have LONG hair."	(x) [(Fx & Bx) → Lx] *or* (x) [Fx → (Bx → Lx)]	Newspaper
"Each PASSENGER was either a DWARF or a MIDGET."	(x) [Px → (Dx ∨ Mx)]	Children's book
"Any CHASE novel is a GOOD novel, as long as its author keeps the story SIMPLE."	(x) [Cx → (Sx → Gx)] *or* (x) [(Cx & Sx) → Gx]	*Newsweek*

The two symbolizations of the second sentence are logically equivalent. The two symbolizations of the fourth sentence exhibit this same pattern and are also equivalent.

These sentences resemble *E* statements:

> No LUTHERAN MECHANICS play CHESS.
> (x) [(Lx & Mx) → ~Cx]
>
> No Lutherans are mechanics who play chess.
> (x) [Lx → ~(Mx & Cx)]

Are the sentences logically equivalent?

Sentences S3 and S4 are similar to *I* statements:

> (S3) (*Newspaper*) "Some newborn BABIES are IRRITABLE and JUMPY."
> (F3) (∃x) [Bx & (Ix & Jx)]
>
> (S4) Some newborn babies who are irritable are also jumpy.
> (F4) (∃x) [(Bx & Ix) & Jx]

S3 and S4 are logically equivalent sentences, and F3 and F4 are equivalent wffs. I propose viewing F5 as an acceptable symbolization of both sentences.

> (F5) (∃x)(Bx & Ix & Jx)

Adopting this relaxation in our punctuation practice will simplify many symbolizations and shorten some proofs. This simplification will be practiced on quantified conjunctions (such as F5) as well as on "unquantified" conjunctions (such as F6).

(F6) Ba & Ia & Ja

A more formal statement of my proposal:

When one of the conjuncts of a (quantified or unquantified) conjunction is itself a conjunction, groupers surrounding the smaller conjunction may be dropped.

Adopting this convention invites a restatement of the Ampersand Out Rule:

The Revised Ampersand Out Rule: From a conjunction, *C*, derive any conjunct of *C* or any conjunction each of whose conjuncts is a conjunct of *C*.

By applying this rule to F6 we may pass in a single step to any wff beneath it in the list.

(F6) Ba & Ia & Ja
       Ba
       Ja & Ba
       Ia & Ba & Ja

We will not alter the Ampersand In Rule.[1]

Some sentences contain more than three predicates. I symbolize four such sentences in the table on p. 50. Examine these symbolizations carefully.

A complicated general sentence can usually be viewed as approximating the pattern of an *A*, *E*, *I*, or *O* statement. Recognizing such a resemblance is an important first step in constructing the symbolization. Consider again the Erma Bombeck sentence:

[All] women with long fingernails [are persons who] never make meat loaf and have husbands who make over $50,000 a year.

If you recognize the *A*-statement pattern you know immediately the overall structure of the symbolization:

(x) [(. . .) → (. . .)]

Symbols representing the grammatical subject are inserted in the first ellipsis and symbols representing the grammatical predicate fill the second ellipsis.

The main connective in a universal quantification is usually the arrow, and the main connective in an existential quantification is generally

[1] We should interpret the Conjunctive Argument and DeMorgan's Law Rules so that they apply to wffs punctuated in accordance with the proposal.

SENTENCE & SYMBOLIZATION	DICTIONARY	SOURCE
"Every TOOTH I have has either been CHIPPED, BROKEN or REPLACED." (x){Tx → [Cx ∨ (Bx ∨ Rx)]}	$Tx = x$ is one of Danny Hodge's teeth	Professional wrestler Danny Hodge
"WOMEN with long FINGERNAILS never make MEAT loaf and have HUSBANDS who make over $50,000 a year." (x)[(Wx & Fx) → (~Mx & Hx)]	$Mx = x$ sometimes makes meat loaf	Erma Bombeck
"PASSENGERS presenting themselves at the airport loading gate LESS than 10 minutes before scheduled departure will not be ACCEPTED if boarding them will DELAY the flight." (x)[(Px & Lx)→(Dx→ ~Ax)]	$Lx = x$ presents himself at the airport loading gate less than 10 minutes before scheduled departure $Dx =$ boarding x delays the flight	Delta ticket envelope
"MISDEMEANOR: a CRIME that is not punishable by DEATH or IMPRISONMENT in a state penitentiary." (x){Mx ↔ [Cx & ~(Dx ∨ Ix)]}	$Dx = x$ is punishable by death $Ix = x$ is punishable by imprisonment in a state penitentiary	Webster

the ampersand. These correlations obtain often enough that it is a wise policy to doublecheck any symbolization that deviates.

Whenever we treat a sentence or an argument in predicate logic, we employ a *universe of discourse*. The universe of discourse is the class of objects over which our quantifiers and variables range. In the preceding chapters our universe of discourse (abbreviated 'UD') has been *everything*.[2] In the succeeding chapters we shall employ this, the largest UD,

[2] The mathematician Georg Cantor established that for every class there is a larger class: the class of its subclasses. Thus talk of a UD consisting of (the class of) *everything* leads to paradox. One way to overcome this difficulty is to employ as the standard UD the class of *everything except classes*. For more on Cantor's paradox, see W. V. Quine, *The Ways of Paradox and other Essays* (New York: Random House, 1966), pp. 3–20 (especially pp. 6–17).

frequently. When our UD is everything, we need not make special reference to it. In some cases we can simplify symbolizations and proofs by using a restricted UD. Let's revert again to the "Bombeck" sentence. When the UD is everything, we must employ the predicates 'is a woman' and 'has long fingernails', but if we restrict our UD to *women* we can drop the first of these predicates and if we further restrict the UD to *women with long fingernails* we eliminate both predicates. Corresponding to these three UD's are three symbolizations of the sentence:

UD: everything   (x) [(Wx & Fx) → (~Mx & Hx)]

UD: women   (x) [Fx → (~Mx & Hx)]

UD: women with long fingernails   (x)(~Mx & Hx)

Wherever a restricted UD is employed in this book, the constitution of that UD will be specified.

Some predicates which may appear to be compound are actually simple; predicate P1 is an example:

(P1)   is a gay activist (that is, campaigns for the rights of homosexuals)

P1 is not equivalent to P2.

(P2)   is gay and an activist

Consider Smith, an activist in the "animal rights" movement and a homosexual not involved in the "gay liberation" movement. Predicate P2 applies to him while P1 does not. P1 is a simple predicate; P2 is compound. Note how the following sentences are symbolized.

Jones is a gay activist.

Bj

Smith is GAY and an ACTIVIST.

Gs & As

(Bx = x is a gay activist)

The *scope* of a quantifier is the portion of the formula that the quantifier governs. The scope is indicated by a pair of groupers (called *quantifier-scope groupers*), the left-hand member of which follows the quantifier. The scope consists of the quantifier plus the quantifier-scope groupers and everything located between those groupers. The scope of the quantifier in F7 is the entire formula, while the scope of the quantifier in F8 is the fragment preceding the arrow.

(F7)   (∃x)(Fx & Gx)

(F8)   (∃x)(Fx & Gx) → Ha

A formal definition of "quantifier scope" is provided in section 10.3. We adopt this formation principle:

A formula is a wff only if each variable in it lies within the scope of a quantifier containing the same variable.

According to this principle, F9 is not a wff, since the last variable lies outside the scope of the quantifier.

(F9) $(\exists x)(Fx \;\&\; Gx) \to Hx$

The symbolization of any English sentence will (if correct) be a wff. Hence F9 cannot symbolize any sentence. Note also that every line in a proof must be a wff.

Quantifier-scope groupers can be eliminated from a wff when their deletion causes no ambiguity. Two types of wffs from which these groupers can be omitted:

(1) a wff in which only one predicate lies within the scope of the quantifier,

(2) a wff in which the first symbol following the quantifier is a tilde.

F10 and F11 are wffs of the first type, and F12 is a wff of the second variety.

(F10) $(\exists x)Fx$

(F11) $(\exists x)Fx \;\&\; Ga$

(F12) $(\exists x) \sim (Fx \;\&\; Gx)$

In Chapter Three the important concepts of "universal quantification" and "existential quantification" were introduced but without adequate definitions. The concept of "scope" was needed for the definitions but was unavailable. The situation can now be rectified.

An *existential quantification* is a wff beginning with an existential quantifier whose scope is the entire wff.

The expression 'universal quantification' is defined analogously. To illustrate the definition above, F8 is not an existential quantification because the scope of its quantifier ends before the arrow.

(F8) $(\exists x)(Fx \;\&\; Gx) \to Ha$

Note that the EO Rule may not be applied to F8 because it is not an existential quantification.

I conclude the section with a table of symbolizations of sample nonstandard statements. The expressions within each box are logically equivalent.

Some Nonstandard Symbolizations

(∃x)Rx	Something is RED.

(∃x)~Rx ~(x)Rx	Something isn't red. Not everything is red.

(x)Rx	Everything is red.

(x)~Rx ~(∃x)Rx	Nothing is red.

(∃x)(Sx ∨ Cx)	Something is either SOLUBLE or COMBUSTIBLE.

(∃x)~(Sx ∨ Cx) (∃x)(~Sx & ~Cx)	Something is neither soluble nor combustible.

(x)(Sx ∨ Cx)	Each thing is either soluble or combustible.
(x)(Sx & Cx)	Everything is both soluble and combustible.
(x)(Sx ↔ Cx)	Each thing is soluble iff it is combustible.
(x)(~Sx → Cx)	Everything insoluble is combustible.
(x)(~Sx → ~Cx)	Nothing insoluble is combustible.

(∃x)(Fx & Rx & Vx)	Some FEMALE REPUBLICANS are VIRGINS. Some females are Republican virgins.

(∃x)(Fx & Rx & ~Vx)	Some female Republicans are not virgins.
(x)[Fx → (Rx & Vx)]	All females are Republican virgins.

(x)[(Fx & Rx) → Vx] (x)[Fx → (Rx → Vx)]	Female Republicans are virgins.

(x)[Fx → (Rx ∨ Vx)]	Females are either Republicans or virgins.
(x)[(Fx ∨ Rx) → Vx]	Females and Republicans are virgins.[3]

(x)[(Fx & Rx) → ~Vx] (x)[Fx → ~(Rx & Vx)]	No female Republicans are virgins. No females are Republican virgins.

5.2
Proofs

We can construct proofs for valid arguments containing nonstandard statements without making *any* modifications in our rules of inference. By way of illustration I will devise proofs for four such arguments. The

---

[3] The symbolization of a sentence of similar form is discussed in exercise 206 at the end of the chapter.

first of these concerns J. M. Duich.[4] Do you think that there *exists* a professor of *turfgrass science*? The following argument settles the matter (given that its premise is true):

J. M. <u>Duich</u> is a professor of TURFGRASS science.

Hence, there exists at least one professor of turfgrass science.

This is one of the simplest arguments that respond to treatment in predicate logic but not in propositional logic. The argument symbolized:

Td $\vdash$ ($\exists$x)Tx

A proof:

(1)	Td	A
(2)	$\sim$($\exists$x)Tx	PA
(3)	(x)$\sim$Tx	2 QE
(4)	$\sim$Td	3 UO
(5)	Td & $\sim$Td	4,1 &I
(6)	($\exists$x)Tx	2-5 $\sim$O

A proposed Constitutional Amendment would permit nondenominational prayer in public schools. Congressman Drinan (the sole Catholic priest in Congress) attacked the proposal with an argument I have paraphrased as follows:

The proposed amendment SANCTIONS only nondenominational prayer. Therefore, since there is no such thing as a nondenominational prayer, the proposed amendment sanctions nothing.[5]

This can be symbolized:

(x)(Sx $\rightarrow$ $\sim$Dx), $\sim$($\exists$x)$\sim$Dx $\vdash$ (x)$\sim$Sx

(UD: prayers; Sx =x is sanctioned by the proposed amendment, Dx =x is denominational) A proof of the argument:

(1)	(x)(Sx $\rightarrow$ $\sim$Dx)	A
(2)	$\sim$($\exists$x)$\sim$Dx	A
(3)	$\sim$(x)$\sim$Sx	PA
(4)	(x)$\sim$$\sim$Dx	2 QE

---

[4] I am indebted to my droll friend Owen Herring for this example, the source of which is the *Williamsport (Pa.) Gazette*.

[5] See William F. Buckley, Jr., "Church Fusses, Misses the Point," *Miami Herald*, November 7, 1971, p. 2–L.

(5) $(\exists x)\sim\sim Sx$ 3 QE

(6) $\sim\sim Sa$ 5 EO

(7) $Sa \rightarrow \sim Da$ 1 UO

(8) $\sim\sim Da$ 4 UO

(9) $\sim Sa$ 7,8 MT

(10) $\sim Sa \ \& \sim\sim Sa$ 9,6 &I

(11) $(x)\sim Sx$ 3–10 $\sim$O

Note that the application of the QE Rule to line 2 results in the wff on line 4 rather than a tilde-free formula. The tildes in line 4 cannot be eliminated by applying the Double Negation Rule to line 4. Why not?

Psychologists at a state prison in Connecticut run a behavior-modification project in which child molesters receive electric shocks while they are shown slides of naked children. In response to criticism of the project, the psychologist in charge claimed that "the program is entirely voluntary." The director of the Connecticut Civil Liberties Union replied:

> *It's inherently coercive — there's no such thing as a real volunteer in a prison, especially when a prisoner knows participating may enhance his chances for parole.*[6]

This criticism summarized:

> No PRISONERS are VOLUNTEERS. Consequently, no prisoners in the BEHAVIOR-modification project are volunteers.

Symbolization and proof:

$(x)(Px \rightarrow \sim Vx) \vdash (x)[(Px \ \& \ Bx) \rightarrow \sim Vx]$

(1) $(x)(Px \rightarrow \sim Vx)$ A

(2) $\sim(x)[(Px \ \& \ Bx) \rightarrow \sim Vx]$ PA

(3) $(\exists x)\sim[(Px \ \& \ Bx) \rightarrow \sim Vx]$ 2 QE

(4) $\sim[(Pa \ \& \ Ba) \rightarrow \sim Va]$ 3 EO

(5) $Pa \rightarrow \sim Va$ 1 UO

(6) $Pa \ \& \ Ba \ \& \sim\sim Va$ 4 AR

(7) $Pa \ \& \sim\sim Va$ 6 &O

(8) $\sim(Pa \rightarrow \sim Va)$ 7 AR

(9) $(Pa \rightarrow \sim Va) \ \& \sim(Pa \rightarrow \sim Va)$ 5,8 &I

(10) $(x)[(Px \ \& \ Bx) \rightarrow \sim Vx]$ 2–9 $\sim$O

---

[6] "Molesters of Children 'Modified' in Prison" and "'There are no Real Volunteers'," *Miami News*, May 21, 1974, p. 8–A.

The wff on line 6 conforms to the relaxed punctuation practice proposed in section 5.1. Line 7 is derived in accordance with the recently liberalized Ampersand Out Rule.

The final example concerns a recently remarried widower, "Nevada," who wrote "Dear Abby" for advice. His bride, Emma, claims that his fourteen-year-old son has been making passes at her, but the boy denies the charge. Abby responds:

> *Dear Nevada: . . . You had better find out for certain who is lying. If Emma is telling the truth, your son needs help. If your son has been unjustly accused, then Emma needs help.*[7]

Her reply suggests this argument:

> If <u>Emma</u> is telling the TRUTH, Nevada's <u>son</u> needs HELP. If she isn't telling the truth, then Emma needs help. Thus, someone needs help.

The argument in symbols:

Te → Hs, ~Te → He ⊢ (∃x)Hx

(UD: people) A proof:

(1)	Te → Hs	A
(2)	~Te → He	A
(3)	~(∃x)Hx	PA
(4)	(x)~Hx	3 QE
(5)	~Hs	4 UO
(6)	~Te	1,5 MT
(7)	He	2,6 →O
(8)	~He	4 UO
(9)	He & ~He	7,8 &I
(10)	(∃x)Hx	3–9 ~O

On occasion, in order to complete a proof you must apply the UO Rule twice to a single universal quantification. This is such a proof; UO is applied twice (at lines 5 and 8) to line 4. Two nonchallenging exercises at the end of this chapter involve "double instantiation."

---

[7] Abigail Van Buren (Chicago Tribune – New York News Syndicate, Inc.), *Miami News*, July 7, 1971, p. 6–C.

EXERCISES

26. Symbolize these statements using the suggested abbreviations.

(a) There are WITCHES.

(b) Nobody's PERFECT. (UD: people)

(c) Some things are unintelligible. ($Ix = x$ is intelligible)

(d) *(Newspaper)* "Not everybody OWNS a color TV set." (UD: people; $Ox = x$ owns a color TV set)

(e) All nonemployees are ELIGIBLE. (UD: people; $Ax = x$ is an employee)

*(f) *(Radio commercial)* "KODAK film — in the one and only YELLOW box." (UD: film; $Kx = x$ is Kodak; $Yx = x$ is in a yellow box)

(g) *(Representative Paul McCloskey, Jr.)* "You can't get on the House Ways and Means COMMITTEE unless you are a GUARDIAN of the oil industry." (UD: Representatives)

*(h) *(Logician Gottlob Frege)* "An OBJECT is anything that is not a FUNC-TION." (This is a definition.)

(i) Some religion PROFESSORS are SKEPTICS or ATHEISTS.

(j) *(Newspaper)* "Every U-M REGULAR has SCORED at least two runs and DRIVEN in at least one." ($Rx = x$ is a U-M regular)

(k) *(Kenyan vice president Moi)* "FOREIGNERS CAUGHT streaking will be DEPORTED in the nude." ($Dx = x$ will be deported in the nude)

(l) *(TV newsman Tom Pettit)* "MORMONS are CHRISTIANS but not PROTESTANTS."

(m) *(Newspaper)* "GREYHOUNDS that can't WIN are DESTROYED."

*(n) *(Children's book)* "HUNGRY CROCODILES SWAM in the river."

(o) *(Logician Geoffrey Hunter)* "A SET is FINITE iff it has only a finite number of MEMBERS." ($Mx = x$ has only a finite number of members)

*(p) *(Disc jockey)* "There are no GOOD-looking WOMEN in BUFFALO."

(q) Not all REPUBLICAN SENATORS are LAWYERS.

(r) *(Newspaper)* "The present law defines a JEW as a 'person who is born of a Jewish MOTHER or who has CONVERTED.'" (UD: people)

*(s) *(Editorialist Anthony Lewis)* "Only a FOOL or a MADMAN could BELIEVE, now, that more bombing will bring peace to Indochina." ($Bx = x$ believes that more bombing will bring peace to Indochina)

(t) *(Sign)* "A lot of fellows who COMPLAIN about their boss being stu-pid would be OUT of a job if the boss were SMART." (UD: people; $Sx = x$'s boss is smart)

*(u) *(Logic text)* "The theorems of S3 are precisely those formulae which

are theorems both of S7 and S4." (UD: formulas; $Ax = x$ is a theorem of S3, $Bx = x$ is a theorem of S7, $Cx = x$ is a theorem of S4)

(v) *(Gen. William Sherman)* "It is only those who have neither FIRED a shot nor HEARD the shrieks and groans of the wounded who CRY aloud for blood, more vengeance, more desolation."

(w) *(Samuel Johnson)* "Every JUDGE who has LAND, trades to a certain extent in corn or in cattle." ($Ax = x$ trades in corn, $Bx = x$ trades in cattle)

*(x) *(Newspaper)* "There are many DOCTORS in the UNITED States who would try HEROIN in terminal care if they could employ it LEGALLY."

(y) *(Malay Mail headline)* "BRA-less WOMEN TOURISTS to be sent PACKING." ($Bx = x$ wears a bra)

27. Translate each wff into a colloquial English sentence using the dictionary provided.

UD: people

$Dx = x$ diets

$Ox = x$ is obese

$Vx = x$ is a vegetarian

(a) $(\exists x)Vx$

*(b) $\sim(x)Ox$

(c) $(x)\sim Ox$

(d) $(\exists x)(Dx \lor Ox)$

*(e) $(x)(Ox \leftrightarrow \sim Vx)$

(f) $(\exists x)(Ox \;\&\; Vx \;\&\; \sim Dx)$

(g) $(x)[Ox \rightarrow (Dx \;\&\; Vx)]$

(h) $(x)[(Ox \;\&\; Dx) \rightarrow Vx]$

Instructions for exercises 28 through 41: Symbolize the arguments and construct proofs for them.

28. Members of the Process Church maintain that Satan is basically good. A spokeswoman, Mother Hathor, argues:

If God created everything, He created Satan as well. And if Satan is a creation of God, then there must be something good about him.[8]

Mother Hathor has two arguments which we can merge into the following:

God CREATED everything. All creations of God are GOOD in some way. So, there is something good about <u>Satan</u>.

($Cx = x$ is a creation of God)

[8] Bob Wilcox, "New Sect Sees Good in Evil," *Miami News*, October 28, 1972, p. 5-B.

29. A letter to the editor:

> *In your Nov. 12 editorial, "Never Forget What's-His-Name," you asserted rashly that no biography has ever been written about Chester A. Arthur, 21st President of the United States. Had you searched a little before going overboard, you would have found that Dodd, Meade & Co., in 1934, published a biography by George Frederick Howe entitled* Chester A. Arthur: A Quarter Century of Machine Politics.
>
> E. F. B. Fries[9]

Fries' argument:

> It is false that no BIOGRAPHY has ever been written about Chester A. Arthur. The proof is that Howe's book is a biography of Arthur.

($Bx = x$ is a biography of Chester A. Arthur, h = Howe's book)

*30. The graffitum below is an argument presented conclusion first. Add this suppressed premise: 'Only those who KNOW you HATE you.' (UD: people; $Kx = x$ knows you, $Hx = x$ hates you)

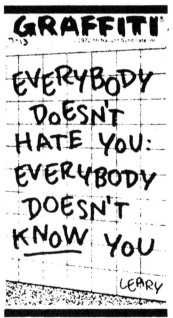

July 13, 1972, McNaught
Syndicate, Inc.

31. In a disturbance at Yosemite National Park, July 4, 1970, youths stoned park rangers and their horses. A park spokesman commented:

> *The Fourth of July weekend confrontation obviously was planned. For instance, some of the chunks of rock thrown at our rangers were sandstone, a variety not found in the park.*[10]

[9] "What's-His-Name Had One Writer," *Miami Herald,* December 26, 1971, p. 6-A.

[10] "Yosemite Denies Brutality Story," *Miami Herald,* August 4, 1970, p. 4-A.

Part of the reasoning involved here may be formalized:

Some of the rocks thrown were SANDSTONE. No sandstone rocks are NATIVE to the park. Any rocks thrown that are not native to the park were BROUGHT in. So, at least some of the thrown rocks were brought to the park.

(UD: rocks thrown during the confrontation)

32. Commenting on one of St. Thomas Aquinas' arguments for the existence of God, the philosopher Etienne Gilson writes:

    . . . The supposition that all beings are merely possible is an absurd one. If not all beings are merely possible, some being must be necessary.[11]

Gilson's argument formalized:

Not all beings are merely POSSIBLE. Each being is either merely possible or it is NECESSARY. Consequently, some being must be necessary.

(UD: beings)

33. At the beginning of the P.T.A. business meeting,[12] the president requested (in English) that the parents who speak only Spanish raise their hands. She was surprised to get no response; but, of course, the result was predictable.

    A person who does not speak only SPANISH won't RAISE his hand. One who does speak just Spanish [won't understand the request and so] won't raise his hand. Therefore, no one will raise his hand.

Ignore the bracketed material when symbolizing. (UD: people attending the meeting; $Sx = x$ speaks only Spanish)

*34. A letter to "Dear Abby":

    In response to your statement that humans are the only animals that blush: You are wrong. Laboratory rats have been trained to blush. . . .

                                                                    R. E. I.: Houston[13]

I formalize the argument:

It is wrong to say that HUMANS are the only ANIMALS that BLUSH. Proof: Some RATS blush. Rats are nonhuman animals.

35. Sports columnist John Crittenden commented on a consequence of the antiblackout legislation passed by Congress in 1973:

    The new blackout policy has put the season ticket holder in a changed and awkward position.
    If he goes to the game, puts out all that money for the fringe expenses and gets baked in the [Miami] sun, there are people who call him sucker.

[11]The Elements of Christian Philosophy (New York: Doubleday & Company, Inc., 1960), p. 79.

[12]The Miami Heights Elementary P.T.A. meeting of March 19, 1974.

[13]Abigail Van Buren (Chicago Tribune-New York News Syndicate, Inc.), Miami News, January 24, 1974, p. 2-B.

He paid the money and they stayed at home and watched the same show
— with instant replay — for nothing. . . .

On the other hand, if the same guy . . . doesn't go to the ball park, but
stays at home and watches on TV with everybody else, all of a sudden
he's a creep.

He's a no-show. According to the propaganda machine of the NFL,
no-shows, whose empty chairs are an embarrassment and who don't pay
the side money which keeps the concessions and the parking lots going,
are going to kill the golden goose.[14]

Crittenden's argument:

Season ticket holders who GO to the game are called SUCKERS. Season ticket holders who don't go are called CREEPS. Thus, season ticket holders are called sucker or creep.

(UD: season ticket holders)

36. In this portion of "Donald Duck and the Mummy's Ring" (1943), the Bey of El Dagga reasons:

Something in the CASES ate FOOD. MUMMIES don't eat. The inhabitants of the cases are mummies or LIVE people. So, there are live people in the cases.

© 1943, Walt Disney Productions.

[14] "The Dolphin Fan is Trapped in the Switch," *Miami News*, October 2, 1973, p. 1-B.

37. A religious tract, "Long Hair: Did Jesus Wear It?" includes this passage:

   Ah, but you say Jesus was a Nazarite and such men did not cut their hair. You are very wrong. . . . There is no scriptural proof Jesus ever took Nazarite vows. Had He done so He could not have drunk grape juice at the last supper (Num. 6:2–4; Mark 14:22–25), nor touched the dead girl (Num. 6:6–7; Mark 5:41). History makes it clear that all other Jews, except those having taken a Nazarite vow, wore short, trimmed hair.[15]

   We can discern this argument:

   NAZARITES never drank GRAPE juice. <u>Jesus</u> drank grape juice. JEWS wore their hair SHORT iff they were not <u>Nazarites</u>. Jesus was Jewish. Hence, Jesus had short hair.

   Some of the premises may be false (the third one for example), but the argument is valid.

38. A letter to George, the wacky advice columnist:

   I have heard that Southerners are polite, Irishmen are imaginative and newspapermen are very literate. I have just met this Southerner who is a

---

[15] Pamphlet written and published by Hal Webb, 508 Buse Street, Ridley Park, Pa.

newspaperman of Irish descent. Don't you think he is a good matrimonial risk?

Hopeful[16]

This argument is suggested by Hopeful's letter:

SOUTHERNERS are POLITE. IRISHMEN are imaginative. NEWSPAPER-MEN are LITERATE. It follows that Southern Irish newspapermen are polite, imaginative, and literate.

($Mx = x$ is imaginative)

*39. When William Merriam, a vice president of ITT, and Congressman Bob Wilson gave conflicting testimony during a Senate Judiciary Committee hearing, Senator Quentin Burdick commented, "Somebody's not telling the truth — take your pick."[17] Burdick's inference:

It is not the case that both <u>Merriam</u> and <u>Wilson</u> are telling the TRUTH. So, somebody's not telling the truth.

(UD: people)

40. In a newspaper column[18] John J. Buckley, the sheriff of Middlesex County, Massachusetts, criticizes the American approach to heroin addiction and praises the British system of governmental distribution of heroin. A paraphrase of his criticism:

In America, heroin ADDICTS are PUSHERS or THIEVES. Pushers CORRUPT the young. Addicted thieves are eventually IMPRISONED. Thus, every American addict is a corrupter of youth or lands in jail or both.

(UD: Americans)

41. Two teams with scrambling quarterbacks (Miami and Dallas) clashed in Super Bowl VI. A few days before the event a Miami sports reporter wrote:

One of pro football's time-honored axioms — a scrambling quarterback will never win a championship — is being exploded here this week. Two of the most mobile and daring quarterbacks in the game are preparing for football's biggest show, Super Bowl VI.

It will be Roger the Dodger versus the Griese Kid's Stuff.

Even the daddy of the scramblers can't sit still waiting for Super Sunday. Fran Tarkenton has been kidding writers in New York this week, "Are they gonna say that you can't win a championship with a drop back passer now?"[19]

[16] "By George!" *Miami News,* June 12, 1971, p. 10-A.

[17] "Feared Memo like Dita's in Files, ITT Man Admits," *Miami News,* April 11, 1972, p. 5-C.

[18] "British Connection," *Miami News,* April 18, 1972, p. 17-A.

[19] Al Levine, "Roger the Dodger Meets Griese Kid," *Miami News,* January 11, 1972, p. 1-C.

The argument beneath the surface of this story has a very unusual logical form:

Either Roger Staubach or Bob Griese will WIN a championship. Since both men are SCRAMBLERS, it follows that the axiom that a scrambling quarterback will never win a championship is mistaken.

(UD: quarterbacks)

204. (CHALLENGING) Symbolize these statements.

(a) *(Sartre)* "All that was not PRESENT did not exist."

(b) *(Lance Rentzel)* "If Pete Rozelle can do this to me [suspend me], he can do this to anyone." (UD: NFL players; Sx = Pete Rozelle can suspend x, r = Lance Rentzel)

(c) *(Joe Paterno)* "If anybody can TURN it [the University of Miami athletic program] around, Ernie McCoy can." (UD: people; $Tx = x$ can turn the UM athletic program around)

(d) *(Newspaper)* "The freeze was LIFTED on all FOOD except BEEF."

(e) *(TV commercial)* "A GREAT hamburger is not a great hamburger without Del Monte CATSUP." (UD: hamburgers)

(f) *(Roadsign in Hell, South Africa)* "Only HELICOPTERS and VOLKS-WAGENS PERMITTED beyond this point."

(g) *(Mark Twain)* "MAN is the only ANIMAL that BLUSHES — or NEEDS to."

(h) *(Letter to Joyce Brothers)* "WOMEN don't have FANTASIES [during sex] unless they are latent LESBIANS or unless they are unhappy with their husbands." ($Hx = x$ is happy with x's husband)

(i) *(Novelist Gerald Kersh)* "Apart from PRIESTS and LAWYERS, anybody who CLAIMS to have had heart-to-heart conversation with Liston is either a VENTRILOQUIST or a liar." (UD: people; $Ax = x$ is a liar)

(j) *(Ben Hecht)* "In HOLLYWOOD, a STARLET is the name for any WOMAN UNDER thirty who is not actively employed in a BROTHEL."

205. (CHALLENGING) A Florida driver's license exam has a multiple-choice question about the meaning of this sign:

The exam key selects the following interpretation as correct:

Left turn from left lane only and traffic in adjoining lane may turn left or continue straight ahead.[20]

Of course, this answer is contradictory. The test constructor confused S1 with S2.

(S1)   Left turns permitted from left lane only.

(S2)   Only left turns permitted from left lane.

Symbolize S1 and S2. (UD: turns; $Lx = x$ is a left turn, $Px = x$ is permitted, $Mx = x$ is made from the left lane)

206. (CHALLENGING) Song title:

(S1)   "RAINY Days and MONDAYS always Get Me DOWN."[21]

A first attempt at symbolizing this title produces F2. (UD: days)

(F2)   (x) [(Rx & Mx) → Dx]

However, a careful reading of F2 shows that it differs in content from S1. F2 symbolizes (the less depressed) S2.

(S2)   Rainy Mondays always get me down.

The song title is properly symbolized by F1.

(F1)   (x) [(Rx → Dx) & (Mx → Dx)]

Provide a wff shorter than F1 (a wff in which no predicate letter occurs twice) which also represents S1. By constructing two proofs establish the logical equivalence of this short formula and F1.

207. (CHALLENGING) A logic puzzle from *Esquire:*[22]

(a) Everyone who WORKS in the I.B.M. Data Dump has SHINGLES.

(b) All HIPPIES are unhappy.

(c) No one whose MOTHER is, or has been, a shaman suffers simultaneously from shingles and mixed DOMINANCE.

(d) Christopher L. Biggleswade works in the I.B.M. Data Dump.

(e) All hippies are fluent in KPELLE and FANG.

(f) Christopher L. Biggleswade is a hippie.

(g) Everyone fluent in Kpelle and Fang is a CANDIDATE for the Doctor's Degree, or else his mother is, or has been, a shaman.

(h) No one who is unhappy can be a candidate for the Ph.D.

Question: Does Biggleswade suffer from mixed dominance? Support your answer with a formal proof. (UD: people; $Ax = x$ is happy, $Mx = x$'s mother is, or has been, a shaman)

----

[20] John Keasler, "Driver's License Exam: No Passing without Failure," *Miami News*, November 23, 1971, p. 8-B. Keasler spotted the error.

[21] Words and music by Paul Williams and Roger Nichols, © Copyright 1970 Almo Music Corp.

[22] © 1971 by Ivan Morris. By permission of the author and Julian Bach Literary Agency, Inc. First published in Esquire Magazine.

208. (CHALLENGING) Formulas F1 and F2 are logically equivalent. F3 and F4 are also logically equivalent. Establish these results by constructing *four* formal proofs. Warning: F2 is not an existential quantification and the EO Rule cannot be applied to it; F4 is not a universal quantification and the UO Rule does not apply to it.

   (F1) (x)(Fx → Ga)

   (F2) (∃x)Fx → Ga

   (F3) (∃x)(Fx → Ga)

   (F4) (x)Fx → Ga

Note that F1 and F4 are not equivalent, nor are F2 and F3. This points up the importance of "quantifier scope." Exercise 219 (Chapter Nine) treats these nonequivalences.

chapter six

Diagrams

6.1
Diagraming Statements

In Chapters Three through Five we have developed a logical technique for establishing the validity of predicate arguments: the method of formal proof. Chapter Six presents a second logical technique, the method of diagrams, which will establish not only validity, but invalidity as well. In the present section I explain how *statements* may be represented in logical diagrams. In the following section I will diagram *arguments* and outline a test of validity (and invalidity) based on argument diagrams.

Statements treated in predicate logic can always be viewed as involving *classes*. Corresponding to each property predicate in the statement will be the class or set of objects to which the predicate can be correctly ascribed. S1, for example, concerns the class of rabbis and the class of Japanese people.

> (S1) Some RABBIS are JAPANESE.

We begin the diagram for S1 (or any *two*-predicate statement) by drawing two overlapping circles within a rectangle.

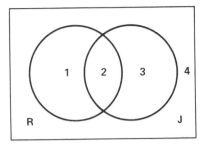

(Numbers are included here to facilitate reference to parts of the diagram; they are not a regular feature of such diagrams.) The diagram consists of four areas or cells which correspond to the four principal subclasses which are determined by two classes. More exactly we have this correspondence:

DIAGRAM CELL	SUBCLASS
1	rabbis who aren't Japanese
2	Japanese rabbis
3	Japanese nonrabbis
4	non-Japanese nonrabbis

S1 may be viewed as expressing the claim that the class of Japanese rabbis has at least one member. We represent membership in a class by placing an X in the cell which corresponds to the class. S1 is diagramed as follows:

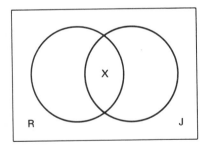

All I statements are diagramed in this way. In most diagrams no marks are made in the area outside all the circles. When no marks are made in the outer cell, the rectangle can be omitted.

S2 is a representative O statement.

(S2)   Some rabbis are not Japanese.

The diagram for S2:

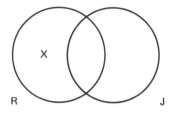

E statements such as S3 are handled differently.

(S3)   No rabbis are Japanese.

S3 does not express the claim that a certain class *has* members; it expresses the opposite claim that the class of Japanese rabbis has *no* members. Clearly we need some device other than the *X* in order to diagram S3. We represent the emptiness of a class by *shading* the cell corresponding to the class. Thus we diagram S3:

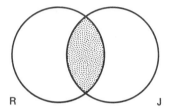

The diagraming of *A* statements (such as S4) is less intuitive than the diagraming of *E, I,* and *O* statements.

(S4)   All rabbis are Japanese.

(S4 is obviously false, but this fact has no relevance to the matter of representing it by diagram.) The correct diagram for the statement:

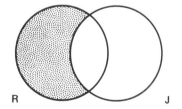

There are several ways to see that this is the appropriate diagram. (i) S4 may be viewed as expressing the claim that any member of the class of rabbis is also a member of the class of Japanese people. The left-hand circle represents the class of rabbis. According to S4 (and speaking loosely) anything which is located in the *R*-circle must reside in that part of the *R*-circle that overlaps the *J*-circle. To indicate this fact we shade the portion of the *R*-circle that lies outside the *J*-circle. By our shading we move all the rabbis over into the class of Japanese. (ii) Once we recognize that S4 expresses a claim of *non*existence, we can rephrase the statement to make this clearer. S4 may be paraphrased as S4′.

    (S4′)   Rabbis who aren't Japanese don't exist.

The diagram in the preceding paragraph is obviously a correct representation of S4′ and hence, also, of S4. (iii) In section 4.1 it was shown that *A* and *O* statements having the same predicates (in the same order) are contradictories. So, S4 and S2 are contradictories.

    (S4)   All rabbis are Japanese.

    (S2)   Some rabbis are not Japanese.

These two statements make exactly opposite claims, and their diagrams will reflect this. To diagram S2 we place an *X* inside the *R*-circle but outside the *J*-circle. To diagram S4 we shade precisely the same area. The S2-diagram claims that a certain class has members; the S4-diagram denies that that class has members.

    When you have mastered the method of diagraming *A*, *E*, *I*, and *O* statements, you will be in a position to diagram most of the statements that occur in predicate arguments one usually encounters outside the logic classroom. Of course, some statements will not be of these standard varieties. Thus, for example, you will be diagraming some one-predicate (or one-class) statements. The diagram for a *one*-predicate statement contains one circle within a box (the latter is often eliminable). Three examples:

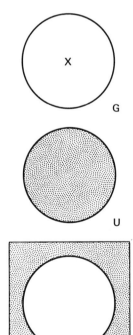

GHOSTS exist.

There are no UNICORNS.

Everything is MATERIAL.

A box is included in the third diagram because marks (in this case *shading*) are inserted outside the circle.

Some *two*-predicate statements are not *A*, *E*, *I*, or *O* statements. I diagram two such sentences.

Some things are neither TASTY nor FATTENING.

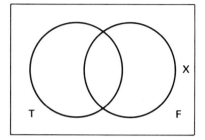

Everything is both tasty and fattening.

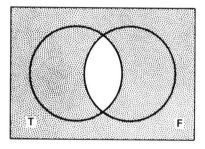

It may be helpful to note that the diagram for a statement whose symbolization is a *universal* quantification always involves shading, while the diagram for a statement which is symbolized by an *existential* quantification contains an *X*.

The basic diagram for a *three*-predicate statement has three overlapping circles. When these circles are enclosed in a rectangle, eight cells result.

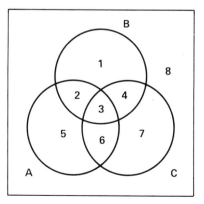

These cells correspond to the eight main subclasses which are determined by three classes, say ARMENIANS, BAKERS, and CATHOLICS.

Cell 1 corresponds to the class of bakers who are neither Armenian nor Catholic; cell 2 represents the class of Armenian bakers who are not Catholic, and so on. Some sample diagrams for *three*-predicate statements:

Some Armenian bakers are not Catholics.

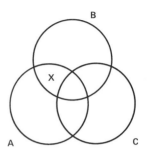

All Armenian bakers are Catholics.

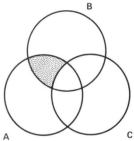

All Armenians are Catholic bakers.

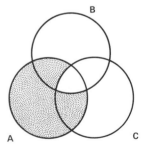

No Armenian bakers are Catholics.

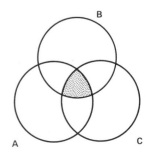

The circles in a logic diagram may be labeled in any order. For example, the top circle in a diagram for the statement 'No Armenian bakers are Catholics' may represent Armenians, bakers, or Catholics.

On occasion, reformulating a sentence may help you see how it should be diagramed. For example, S5 can be rephrased as S6, and the latter sentence is probably easier to diagram.

> (S5) All Armenian bakers are Catholics.
>
> (S6) There are no non-Catholic Armenian bakers.

Of course, it is essential that the reformulated sentence be logically equivalent to the original sentence. Symbolization may help you determine logical equivalence.

> (S5) All Armenian bakers are Catholics.
>
> (F5) (x) [(Ax & Bx) → Cx]
>
> $\sim$($\exists$x)$\sim$ [(Ax & Bx) → Cx]
>
> $\sim$($\exists$x)(Ax & Bx & $\sim$Cx)
>
> (F6) $\sim$($\exists$x)($\sim$Cx & Ax & Bx)
>
> (S6) There are no non-Catholic Armenian bakers.

F5 is a proper symbolization of S5, and F6 correctly symbolizes S6. If one realizes that each of the first three wffs in this list is logically equivalent to the wff beneath it, one will be satisfied that S5 and S6 are equivalent.

Some statements assert existence in *one or another* of several subclasses. To represent such a statement we place an *X* in each cell involved and connect the *X*'s with lines. For example:

Some Armenians are either bakers or Catholics (or both).

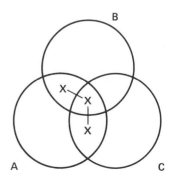

This diagram does not assert existence in *each* of three subclasses but in *at least one* of three subclasses.

Four classes determine sixteen main subclasses. It is a theorem of topology that no diagram formed of four circles in a box will satisfactorily represent these subclasses.[1] So, in order to accommodate *four*-predicate statements we must adopt a different type of diagram:

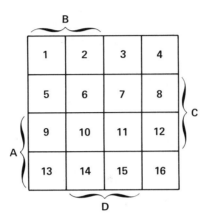

Each main class is represented in this diagram by a rectangle composed of eight cells. Corresponding to the class of Armenians, for example, is the rectangle composed of cells 9 through 16; corresponding to the class of bakers is the rectangle consisting of cells 1, 2, 5, 6, 9, 10, 13, and 14. One cell (4) in this diagram represents individuals who belong to none of the four main classes; hence a box surrounding the diagram is never required.

I will diagram two four-predicate statements:

[1]A diagram of four overlapping *ovals* can be drawn:

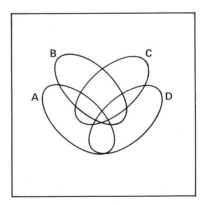

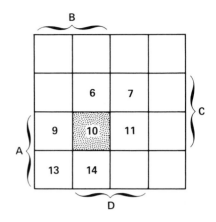

No Armenian bakers are
Catholic DART-throwers.

Armenian bakers are represented in the diagram by the square composed of cells 9, 10, 13, and 14, while Catholic dart-throwers are represented by the square composed of cells 6, 7, 10, and 11. The cell common to both squares is shaded. A second example:

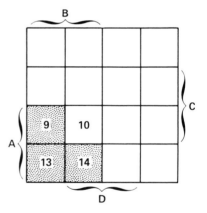

Every Armenian baker
is a Catholic
dart-thrower.

Catholic dart-throwers can "inhabit" only one of the four cells (9, 10, 13, and 14) which represent the class of Armenian bakers, namely, cell 10. So, the other three cells are shaded. Diagrams can be constructed for statements containing more than four predicates, but I shall not deal with such diagrams in this book.[2]

---

[2] For more on logic diagrams see Martin Gardner, *Logic Machines and Diagrams* (New York: McGraw-Hill Book Company, Inc., 1958). The circle diagrams were devised by John Venn around 1881; rectangular diagrams were invented by Allan Marquand at the same time.

The final topic of the section is the diagraming of *singular state-ments*. A lower-case letter (a *name*) represents an individual. An example:

Shakespeare was not GAY.

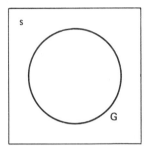

A statement which asserts that an individual belongs to *one or another* of several subclasses may be diagramed by placing a name in each of the appropriate cells and connecting the various letters with lines. An illustration:

Shakespeare was gay or
FEMALE but not both.

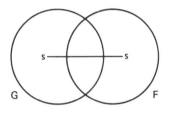

6.2
Testing Arguments

Now that we know how to diagram *statements*, it is a small additional step to diagraming *arguments*. First draw a basic diagram with one circle (or rectangle) for each predicate in the argument. Then diagram each premise—but not the conclusion. For illustration I will diagram the "bus" argument from Chapter One:

All SCHOOL buses are YELLOW.

No GREEN buses are yellow.

Thus, no green buses are school buses.

The basic diagram contains three circles. After I represent the first premise, the diagram appears:

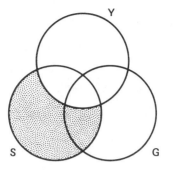

The first premise concerns the classes of school buses and yellow objects. In shading the diagram I attend to the S-circle and the Y-circle and ignore the G-circle. Next I diagram the second premise:

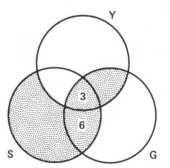

The diagram is now complete and we are ready to test the argument for validity, employing the following principle:

The argument is valid iff the conclusion is represented in the diagram.

You would diagram the conclusion of the "bus" argument by shading cells 3 and 6. They are both shaded in the diagram above. Hence, we know the argument to be valid.

Our second sample argument is the "ape" argument, also from Chapter One:

All MAMMALS have HAIR.

All APES have hair.

Therefore, all apes are mammals.

The premises diagramed:

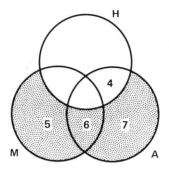

The first premise requires shading of cells 5 and 6, while the second involves shading cells 6 and 7. Is the conclusion represented in the diagram? If we were to diagram the conclusion, we would shade cells 4 and 7. Since one of those cells is not shaded, the diagram does not represent the conclusion. We judge the argument *invalid*. By studying the diagram you can determine not only *that* the argument is invalid but also *why* it is invalid. The diagram reveals that it is quite consistent with the two premises that there be hairy apes who aren't mammals (see cell 4). The conclusion, however, denies that there are such apes, so the conclusion makes a claim which goes beyond the premises. In a valid deductive argument the conclusion never claims more than the premises. Logic diagrams often bolster our logical insight.

A third argument for testing:

> Every QUAKER is RELIGIOUS.
> Some Quakers are ATHEISTS.
> So, some atheists are religious.

We diagram the premises:

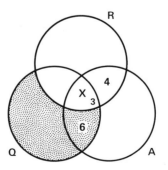

When we diagram premise one, we shade cell 6 (and another cell). Premise 2 claims membership in one or another of the subclasses which are represented by cells 3 and 6. Since cell 6 has been shaded, the X must be located in the remaining cell, 3. The X in cell 3 makes the claim that at least one atheist is religious—the claim made by the conclusion. Hence, the argument is valid.

A puzzling feature of this example requires discussion. If we were to diagram the conclusion of the "Quaker" argument, we would place X's in both cells 3 and 4 and connect them with a line. We would place an X in cell 3 alone in order to diagram S1:

(S1) Some atheist Quakers are religious.

S1 is a more specific statement than the conclusion of the "Quaker" argument, but it plainly *entails* the conclusion. Since S1 follows from the premises of the argument, so does the conclusion. I reformulate the testing principle to accommodate such cases:

The argument is valid iff the conclusion is entailed by the information represented by the diagram.

An important procedural principle:

Do all shading before entering X's (or names).

I can show the point of this principle by violating it as I re-diagram the "Quaker" argument. Premise two asserts membership in the class associated with cells 3 and 6; I diagram it by inserting connected X's in those two cells:

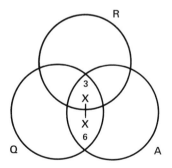

Then I complete the diagram by representing premise one.

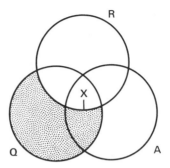

One of the X's and half the connecting line have been shaded over. This diagram is confusing at best. If you adopt the procedural principle stated above, you will avoid such confusing diagrams.

A discussion of the military draft in the magazine *Ms.* includes the comment that "as long as Congress intends to draft citizens, and women are citizens, women will be drafted."[3] Is the author thinking in terms of this syllogism?

> Some CITIZENS are DRAFTED.
>
> All American WOMEN are citizens.
>
> Hence, some American women are drafted.

I diagram premise two:

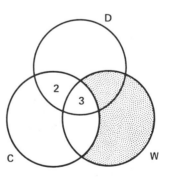

Premise one claims membership in the class associated with cells 2 and 3. Notice that the premise does not indicate which of these two cells has members. It would be a serious mistake, therefore, to place an X (unconnected with other X's) in cell 2, and it would also be an error to place an X (unconnected with other X's) in cell 3. To insert a free-standing X in either of these cells would be to include in the diagram information more

[3] Ann Scott, "The Equal Rights Amendment: What's in it for You?" July, 1972, p. 85.

specific than that provided by premise one. The premise is correctly diagramed by inserting *connected* X's in cells 2 and 3. The significance of
the connected X's is that there is membership in one or the other (and
possibly both) of the two classes associated with cells 2 and 3.

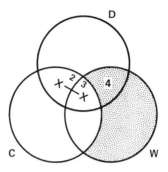

This diagramming represents exactly the information supplied by the
first premise. Is the argument valid? The conclusion claims membership
in the class associated with cells 3 and 4. As cell 4 has been shaded, the
conclusion would be represented by an X in cell 3 *which was not connected with other X's*. The diagram above does not represent the conclusion (or anything that entails the conclusion); thus, the syllogism is
invalid.

Perhaps the author of the *Ms.* quotation had in mind this syllogism:

Some citizens are drafted.
Some citizens are women.
Hence, some women are drafted.

Diagramed:

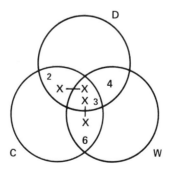

The connected X's in cells 2 and 3 are compatible with the emptiness of
the class associated with cell 3, and the connected X's in cells 3 and 6 do
not imply membership in the class corresponding to cell 3. Therefore,
the diagram does *not* claim membership in the class associated with

cells 3 and 4, and so does not represent the conclusion. The syllogism is invalid.

The philosopher David Hume writes:

> All ideas are borrow'd from preceding PERCEPTIONS. Our ideas of OBJECTS, therefore, are deriv'd from that source.[4]

In diagraming arguments, just as in symbolizing them, we may employ a restricted UD. Since the premise and conclusion of Hume's argument concern ideas, we are free to restrict our universe to ideas. The P-circle will represent the class of ideas derived from perceptions, while the O-circle stands for the class of ideas of objects. The premise is diagramed as follows:

UD: ideas

(I include beside the diagram a specification of the restricted UD.) Note that it is necessary to shade both cells 3 and 4. Because cell 3 is shaded, the diagram represents the conclusion; hence, we judge the argument valid.

A news story written shortly before Pope Paul's 75th birthday concerned the possibility of his imminent abdication. The last paragraph of the story:

> There have been recurrent rumors about a possible resignation since 1966, when he [Pope Paul] told Roman Catholic bishops around the world to hand in their resignations when they reach 75. By tradition, the Pope also is bishop of Rome.[5]

These rumors were based on an argument:

All BISHOPS should RESIGN when they reach 75.

Pope Paul is a bishop.

So, he should resign when he reaches 75.

---

[4] A Treatise of Human Nature (Oxford: The Clarendon Press, 1888), p. 634.

[5] "Pope Talks of Quitting, but Won't," Miami News, May 31, 1972, p. 2-A.

The diagram:

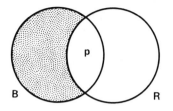

This argument is valid.

The last argument I shall diagram in this section was advanced by consumer advocate Bess Myerson Grant (as recounted in a newspaper story):

> *Mrs. Grant pointed out that filet mignon is not a kosher cut of meat. . . .*
> *She said federal regulations define filet mignon as beef prepared from*
> *the hind quarter. Jewish dietary laws forbid eating meat cut from the*
> *hind quarter of any animal.*[6]

Her argument formalized:

All FILET mignon is BEEF cut from the HIND-quarter. No hind-quarter cuts are KOSHER. It follows that no filet mignon is kosher.

(UD: cuts of meat) A 16-cell diagram is required:

UD: cuts of meat

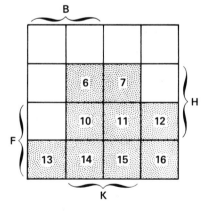

The first premise *(All F is B-H)* is diagramed by shading cells 11 through 16 — the cells in F but not in *both* B and H. The second premise *(No H are K)* is diagramed by shading cells 6, 7, 10, and 11. The conclusion *(No F is K)* is represented, since cells 10, 11, 14, and 15 have all been shaded.

[6] "Caterers Rapped for Unkind Cuts," *Miami Herald,* October 24, 1970, p. 9-A.

There are predicate arguments which lie beyond the scope of the logic-diagram technique explained in this chapter, but it applies to a very large group of arguments, including most of the predicate arguments one encounters outside the logic classroom. The technique has several virtues: (i) it establishes invalidity as well as validity, (ii) it can increase insight into the structure of the arguments examined, and (iii) it does not require symbolization of the arguments tested (and so could be employed by someone even after he had forgotten how to symbolize predicate statements).

EXERCISES

42. Diagram each statement.

    (a) Something is RED.

    *(b) Something isn't red.

    (c) Nothing is red.

    (d) <u>Arthur</u> is FAT.

    (e) <u>Bertha</u> is not fat.

    *(f) <u>Carl</u> is TALL but not fat.

    (g) Something is neither SOLUBLE nor COMBUSTIBLE.

    (h) Something is either soluble or combustible or both.

    (i) Nothing is either soluble or combustible.

    (j) All FEMALES are REPUBLICAN VIRGINS.

    *(k) All females are Republicans or virgins or both.

    (l) All female Republicans are virgins.

    (m) Some ARMENIAN BOSTONIANS are CATHOLIC DENTISTS.

    *(n) All Armenian Bostonian Catholics are dentists.

43. In section 4.1 it was explained that I statements are validly convertible. That is, for example, S1 and S2 are logically equivalent.

    (S1) Some RABBIS are JAPANESE.

    (S2) Some Japanese are rabbis.

E statements are also validly convertible; S3 is equivalent to S4.

    (S3) No CONSERVATIVES are NUDISTS.

    (S4) No nudists are conservatives.

However, A statements and O statements cannot be validly converted. S5 is not equivalent to S6; nor are S7 and S8 equivalent.

    (S5) All "UPPERS" are DRUGS.

    (S6) All drugs are "uppers."

    (S7) Some REPTILES are not SNAKES.

(S8) Some snakes are not reptiles.

Construct four diagrams to demonstrate that

(a) S1 entails S2;

(b) S3 entails S4;

(c) S5 does not entail S6;

(d) S7 does not entail S8.

Instructions for exercises 44 through 55: Evaluate each argument by construct-ing a diagram; label the argument valid *or* invalid. *(Arguments need not be symbolized.)*

*44. A Vega advertisement reads in part:

> *But a good little car should get you from here to there without your feel-ing every mile in between. And Vega does.*

The copywriter wants the reader to infer that Vega is a GOOD little car. Check this argument. (UD: little cars; $Hx = x$ will get you from here to there without your feeling every mile in between)

45. In the third panel of the "Andy Capp" comic strip on page 86, Andy draws a conclusion from two of his own statements:

> Only IDIOTS are POSITIVE. Andy is positive.

Supply the unstated conclusion.

46. I reviewed a manuscript for a logic textbook which included this argument:

> The argument pattern *modus ponens* CORRESPONDS to a tautology. This discovery tells us that every valid truth-functional argument pattern corresponds to some tautology or other.

(UD: valid truth-functional argument patterns; $m = modus\ ponens,\ Cx = x$ corresponds to some tautology)

47. When the late J. Edgar Hoover was asked (during a congressional hearing in 1972) whether gay activists were allowed in the FBI, he responded:

> *We don't allow any types of activists in the FBI, gay or otherwise.*[7]

Hoover's reply was an argument:

> No ACTIVISTS are FBI agents. GAY activists are activists. Hence, no gay activists are FBI agents.

($Fx = x$ is an FBI agent, $Gx = x$ is a gay activist)

48. A philosophy doctoral dissertation contains this argument:

> Any statement is CONTRADICTORY if it ENTAILS two statements such that one of the latter is the denial of the other. No NEGATIVE existential

---

[7] "'Hippies, Gays and Activists' Are on FBI's Not-wanted List," *Miami News,* April 28, 1972, p. 11-A.

statement entails statements one of which is the denial of the other. Consequently, no negative existential statement is contradictory.

(UD: statements; $Ex = x$ entails two statements one of which is the denial of the other, $Nx = x$ is negative existential)

49. A minor scandal in Miami concerned former city employees receiving total disability pensions who now work full-time for other employers.[8] This syllogism summarizes the issue:

    No full-time WORKER is totally DISABLED. Some of those receiving total disability PENSIONS from the City of Miami work full-time. So, some recipients of these pensions are not totally disabled.

50. A newspaper feature story on the judiciary in South Florida begins:

    In Dade County the trend is not the ballot box but death, retirement or scandal that usually determines who the more than 70 court judges will be.

    Though bench seats are elective offices, it's taboo among attorneys — and they're the only ones eligible to be judges — to run against an incumbent judge.

    Therefore, weak or mediocre judges often occupy a bench seat for decades.[9]

This argument is suggested:

    ATTORNEYS will not CHALLENGE an incumbent judge. Being an attorney is a necessary condition for challenging an incumbent judge. It follows that no one challenges an incumbent judge.

($Cx = x$ challenges an incumbent judge)

51. A newspaper editorial:

    The president of the American Bar Association has come out foursquare in favor of ethical behavior for lawyers. Or has he?

    Chesterfield Smith, speaking of the Watergate scandal at a Cincinnati press conference, said "we want to purge from our profession any crooks who are unworthy of our high profession."

    It follows, then, that there are some crooks worthy? Mr. Smith should provide guidelines.[10]

The editorial (which is probably intended as a joke) suggests that S1 entails S2. Does it?

(S1) Any CROOKS who are unworthy of the legal profession DESERVE to be purged from the profession.

(S2) Some crooks are WORTHY to be lawyers.

(UD: lawyers)

[8] Tom Brandt, "Pension Board Weighs Changes," *Miami News*, May 4, 1974, pp. 1-A and 3-A.

[9] Tom Brandt, "Death, Scandal Decide Judges," *Miami News*, August 12, 1974, p. 6-A.

[10] "How Worthy?" *Miami News*, October 13, 1973, p. 14-A.

°52. Paragraph of a history textbook:

> *The Berlin Decree, issued by Napoleon in November 1806, forbade all trade with the British Isles and all commerce in British merchandise. It ordered the arrest of all Britons on the Continent and the confiscation of their property. Britain replied by requiring that neutral vessels wishing to trade with France put in first at a British port and pay duties. . . . Napoleon retaliated with the Milan Decree (December 1807), ordering the seizure of all neutral ships that complied with the new British policy. The neutrals, in effect, were damned if they did and damned if they didn't.*[11]

The dilemma of the neutral shippers is summarized by this argument:

Neutral ships which COMPLIED with Britain's policy were in trouble with FRANCE. Neutral ships which failed to comply were in trouble with BRITAIN. So, every netural ship was in trouble with France or with Britain.

(UD: neutral ships)

53. A book review begins:

> *[Bleep's] goal is to establish that men are free. His central argument is that (1) any machine is incapable of being free; (2) that any machine is logically incapable of detecting, or constructing proofs of, certain true statements [Goedel statements] that men can detect as being true. . . .*[12]

A formalization of this argument:

No MACHINES are FREE. No machine can DETECT Goedel statements. Some HUMANS can detect Goedel statements. This establishes that at least some men are free.

°54. From a news story:

> *[Maria Medina's] . . . house was burglarized while she was away for a few hours.*
> *"They took my TV, and I knew they must have been Cubans, because they even took my Saint Lazarus (an image of a Catholic saint) with the candle I had lit for him and the glass of water and everything—Americans don't believe in all that."*[13]

Maria's argument formalized:

Someone took the TELEVISION and the St. LAZARUS icon. No native AMERICAN would steal the icon. Whoever took the TV was native American or CUBAN. Therefore, some Cuban stole the TV.

(UD: people; $Tx = x$ took the television, $Lx = x$ took the St. Lazarus icon)

55. Until recently (when it was killed by school administrators), the University

---

[11] Crane Brinton, John B. Christopher, and Robert Lee Wolf, *A History of Civilization* (Englewood Cliffs, N.J.: Prentice-Hall, Inc., 1971), p. 694.

[12] *Choice*, June 1971, p. 560.

[13] Hilda Inclan, "'I Signed Away Kids, Influence Was Bad'," *Miami News*, May 9, 1974, p. 6-A.

of Miami had a student-founded community-service program called "Summon." The following passage from a story in the college newspaper details one of the problems Summon faced:

> ... *SUMMON is offered only as a credit-only course. However, the University permits a student to take only one credit-only course per semester.* ...
>
> *Freshmen, however, almost to a man, must exercise their single credit-only option for the required English courses, 101-102. Hence the entire frosh class is prohibited from entering the SUMMON course.*[14]

The argument contained in this passage may be paraphrased as follows:

> Students who take both SUMMON and ENGLISH 101-102 take (at least) TWO credit-only courses. No student takes two credit-only courses. Every FRESHMAN takes English 101-102. So, no freshman takes Summon.

(UD: University of Miami students)

209. (CHALLENGING) Section 2.2 begins:

> *Let's define a SINGULAR statement as a statement CONTAINING one or more singular terms. We shall call a statement that has no singular terms a GENERAL statement. (Does it follow from these definitions that every statement is either singular or general? Do the definitions imply that no statement is both?)*

Answer the two questions with the aid of a diagram. (UD: statements)

210. (CHALLENGING) (a) Exercise 40 (Chapter Five) has five predicates. Devise a diagram for five-predicate arguments and use it to demonstrate the validity of argument 40. (b) Assess this argument by (five-class) diagram:

> No EXISTENTIAL statement is ANALYTIC. Every analytic statement is *a PRIORI*. Every statement is analytic or SYNTHETIC; none are both. There are NECESSARY existential statements. It follows that some synthetic *a priori* statements are necessary.

(UD: statements) (c) Devise a diagram for six-predicate arguments and use it to demonstrate the validity of exercise 38 (Chapter Five).

211. (CHALLENGING) Establish the validity of this argument by constructing a formal proof.

> Dean is ARMENIAN. He is also a BAPTIST. Hence, there are Armenian Baptists.

Test the argument by diagram. If you find that the diagram test yields the verdict "invalid," suggest some alteration in the test so that it will assess the argument "valid."

---

[14]Norman Manasa, "SUMMON Program 'Stoned' by UM's Administrative 'Gods'," *Miami Hurricane,* January 11, 1972, p. 4.

chapter seven

Existential Import

7.1
Penevalid Arguments

A children's book on magnets includes this passage:

> *The magnet won't even pick it [the penny] up from his hand. Magnets won't pick up pennies, dry or wet! But aren't pennies made of metal?*[1]

The authors are encouraging children to draw this inference:

PENNIES are not ATTRACTED by magnets. Pennies are made of METAL. Hence, some metallic objects are not attracted by magnets.

Intuitively, we judge this argument *valid*. But a surprise awaits us when we test it by the diagram method:

---

[1] Franklyn M. Branley and Eleanor K. Vaughan, *Mickey's Magnet* (New York: Scholastic Book Services, 1956), p. 27.

[2] Since the claim made by the conclusion is not made by the premises, it (and, hence, the conclusion also) may be false although the premises are true. If it is possible for the premises of an argument to be true and the conclusion false, the argument is invalid.

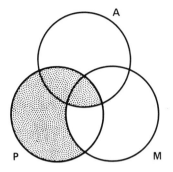

The diagram includes no X; the conclusion is not represented. How is this anomaly to be explained?

Recall that we diagram I and O statements by inserting X's. The significance of placing an X in a cell is that there *exists* a member of the class corresponding to that cell. Logicians interpret I and O statements as claiming the existence of something; in technical jargon, logicians accord *existential import* to such statements. A and E statements, by contrast, are diagramed by shading and not by placing X's. The significance of shading a cell is that the class in question has no members. Most logicians regard A and E statements as lacking existential import. If the conclusion of an argument makes a claim that is not made by the premises, then the argument is invalid. (Why?)[2] It follows that an argument whose premises lack existential import but whose conclusion has existential import will be an invalid argument. And so most logicians will judge *invalid* any argument whose premises are exclusively A or E statements and whose conclusion is an I or an O statement. The "magnet" argument is of this type.

Arguments of the "magnet" variety may be called *penevalid,* that is, "almost valid." A penevalid argument is one which becomes valid when the proper (one-predicate) existential premise is added. The premise that does the trick for the "magnet" argument is 'There are pennies' (or 'Pennies exist'). Adding this premise alters the diagram:

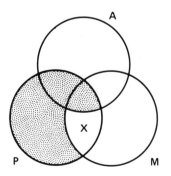

The conclusion is now represented. Note that adding the premise 'There are metallic objects' does not suffice; see the diagram below.

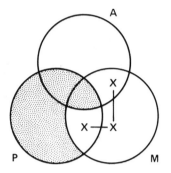

Adding the premise 'There are objects attracted by magnets' also fails to transform the original argument into a valid one.

The method of formal proofs and the method of diagrams conform on this point. A proof of the original two-premised "magnet" argument is not possible,[3] but a proof can be completed when 'There are pennies' is added to the premises.

(1)	$(x)(Px \rightarrow \sim Ax)$	A
(2)	$(x)(Px \rightarrow Mx)$	A
(3)	$(\exists x)Px$	A (the existential premise)
(4)	$\sim(\exists x)(Mx \& \sim Ax)$	PA
(5)	$(x)\sim(Mx \& \sim Ax)$	4 QE
(6)	Pa	3 EO
(7)	Pa $\rightarrow \sim$Aa	1 UO
(8)	Pa $\rightarrow$ Ma	2 UO
(9)	$\sim$(Ma & $\sim$Aa)	5 UO
(10)	$\sim$Aa	7,6 $\rightarrow$O
(11)	Ma	8,6 $\rightarrow$O
(12)	$\sim$Ma	9,10 CA
(13)	Ma & $\sim$Ma	11,12 &I
(14)	$(\exists x)(Mx \& \sim Ax)$	4–13 $\sim$O

Let's describe a subject-predicate statement as having *existential import* when it entails the nonemptiness of its subject class. (The *subject class* is the class corresponding to its grammatical subject.) As mentioned above, the standard position in logic is to regard I and O statements as having existential import and A and E statements as lacking

---

[3] But remember that failure to construct a proof does not *establish* invalidity.

such import. For example, S1 is viewed as entailing S3, while S2 is held not to entail S3.

(S1) Some pines are conifers.

(S2) All pines are conifers.

(S3) There are pines.

The denial of existential import to S2 was implicit in the paraphrase S2′ provided in section 2.3.

(S2′) For any individual, *if* it is a pine, *then* it is a conifer.

It is obvious that S2′ does not claim that pines exist. However, we could have offered S4 as a paraphrase of S2:

(S4) Pines exist, and if any individual is a pine, then it is a conifer.

S4 is symbolized by F4.

(F4) (∃x)Px & (x)(Px → Cx)

If we symbolized S2 by F4, we would be according existential import to S2. Had we viewed S2 in this way, we would have diagramed it as follows:

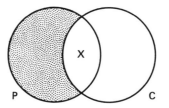

A diagram for the original "magnet" argument drawn in accordance with this proposal would represent the conclusion. A logician who accords existential import to A and E statements will judge the original "magnet" argument valid, not merely penevalid.

I have shown that logicians *could* regard A statements as having existential import. Why don't they? There are two main reasons. First, some natural-language A statements clearly lack existential import. S5 and S6 are examples:

(S5) Any make-up exams given will be orals.

(S6) Every moving body subject to no outside forces continues to move in a straight line.

S5 does not entail S7.

(S7)   Some make-up exams will be given.

S5 expresses a teacher's policy and it need not be withdrawn on the subsequent discovery that S7 is false. S6 does not entail S8, for S6 is true and S8 false.

(S8)   Some moving bodies are subject to no outside forces.

S5 and S6 are A statements that should not be symbolized or diagramed existentially. Treating all A statements alike simplifies logic considerably. If some A statements ought not to be regarded existentially, then perhaps none should be so regarded. This argument is strengthened by pointing out that no A statements *must* be regarded existentially. Let's recur to S2 for an example.

(S2)   All pines are conifers.

A person who asserts S2 is *assuming* that pines exist, but it isn't clear that in uttering S2 he is *asserting* that they exist. If S2 has existential import, then anyone who utters it *is* asserting two propositions: (a) "Pines exist," and (b) "(If there are pines) each pine is a conifer." It seems doubtful that in uttering S2 one must be making these two claims.

There is a second reason why most logicians do not accord existential import to A statements. They regard A and O statements (containing the same predicates in the same order) as contradictories, and they accord existential import to O statements. These two views lead to the denial that A statements have existential import. In explaining why this is so it will be useful to think about these three statements:

(S9)   All unicorns are herbivores.
(S10)   Some unicorns are not herbivores.
(S11)   There are unicorns.

Any statement which entails a false statement is itself false. S10 entails S11 (according to many logicians) and S11 is false; therefore, S10 is false. S9 and S10 are contradictories (so logicians generally maintain); hence, they must have opposite truth values. Since they have opposite truth values and since S10 is false, S9 must be true. S9 is true and S11 is false; it follows that S9 does not entail S11. Therefore (on the standard view), S9 lacks existential import. (I have been concentrating on the thesis that A statements lack existential import. Similar remarks will apply to E statements.)

The decision to ascribe existential import to I and O statements but not to A and E statements has some unhappy consequences. For example, this decision forces us to catalogue the original "magnet" argument as only *pene*valid, when it seems so obviously valid. Nevertheless, this position is superior to the one which ascribes existential import to *A* and *E* statements. Incidentally, only a very small portion of the arguments you encounter would have their assessment affected by decisions about existential import. And when you do come across such an argument, it is a simple matter to add the required existential premise.

Under the standard interpretation, an *A* statement does not entail the *I* statement containing the same predicates in the same order, nor does an *E* statement entail the corresponding *O* statement. For example, S2 does not entail S1 (and F2 does not entail F1).

(S2)	All pines are conifers.	(F2)	(x)(Px → Cx)
(S1)	Some pines are conifers.	(F1)	(∃x)(Px & Cx)

Some people believe (perhaps through generalizing too hastily from examples such as the above) that *no* universal quantification entails *any* existential quantification; this, however, is a mistake. F12 entails F3, a fact one can easily demonstrate by formal proof.

(F12)	(x)Px	(S12)	Everything is a pine.
(F3)	(∃x)Px	(S3)	There are pines.

EXERCISES

Instructions for exercises 56 through 59: Each argument is penevalid. By constructing a diagram discover the (one-predicate) existential premise that converts it into a valid argument. Symbolize the strengthened argument and construct a formal proof. Note that the proof can be completed only with the aid of the existential premise.

*56.   All CONIFERS are PINES. Hence, some conifers are pines.

57.   All the area COORDINATORS attended the BANQUET. Everyone at the banquet made a PLEDGE. Thus, some of those who pledged are area coordinators.

58.   PREPOSITIONS aren't NAMES. Prepositions are MEANINGFUL. This shows that some meaningful words are not names.

This syllogism has point because some philosophers have held that every meaningful word is a name.

59.   A philosopher visiting the University of Miami organized a talk to the philosophy club around this argument:

All PHYSICAL events can be explained in purely physical TERMS. No event of EXTRA-sensory perception is explainable in purely physical terms. Every ESP event is a MENTAL event. Therefore, some mental events are not physical events.

212. (CHALLENGING) A peculiarity of the standard account of A statements is revealed in the fact that S1 entails S2.

(S1)   There are no GHOSTS.

(S2)   All ghosts are MATHEMATICIANS.

Demonstrate this entailment, first by diagram and then by formal proof. The comic strip below may be viewed as involving an argument of this odd sort:

There are no moose (in the camp). So, all the moose (in the camp) are counted by Ira.

July 15, 1971, Field Enterprises, Inc.

213. (CHALLENGING) Among arguments where both diagram and formal-proof techniques are applicable, the two techniques give consistent results with very few exceptions. Find an exception: an argument which is assessed *valid* by formal proof but just *penevalid* by diagram. Test it by both techniques. How could the diagram test be altered to make the two techniques conform more closely?

chapter eight

Multiple Quantification

8.1
Symbolization

I will call a wff containing more than one quantifier a *multiple quantification.* An example:

(x)Ax ∨ (∃x)Bx

A wff with one quantifier is termed a *unary quantification.* In preceding chapters we worked with unary quantifications and wffs without quantifiers. In this chapter we treat multiple quantifications — but not multiple quantifications of all types. We will concentrate on those whose predicates are all *property* predicates; multiple quantifications containing *relational* predicates are discussed in Chapter Ten. The present section concerns the *symbolization* of sentences with multiply quantified wffs. Section 8.2 treats *proofs* of symbolized arguments which involve multiple quantifications.

Many multiple quantifications consist of two unary quantifications joined by a dyadic statement connective (an arrow, ampersand, wedge, or double arrow). Statement S1 is symbolized by such a wff.

(S1)   If some BOTTLES are RECYCLABLE, then all bottles can be recycled.

(F1) $(\exists x)(Bx \,\&\, Rx) \rightarrow (x)(Bx \rightarrow Rx)$

S1 is a conditional whose antecedent is an *I* statement and whose consequent is an *A*. More examples:

Either everything is MENTAL or everything is PHYSICAL.
$(x)Mx \lor (x)Px$

There are BORROWERS iff there are LENDERS.
$(\exists x)Bx \leftrightarrow (\exists x)Lx$

(Newspaper) "Someone is going to get KILLED unless someone FIXES the lightpole." (UD: people)
$\sim(\exists x)Fx \rightarrow (\exists x)Kx$

The term 'any' (or 'anyone') is ordinarily symbolized by a universal quantifier, but there are exceptions. S2 is correctly symbolized by F2.

(S2)   If anyone passed the EXAM, someone will THROW a party.

(F2) $(\exists x)Ex \rightarrow (\exists x)Tx$

(UD: people) When 'any' occurs in the antecedent of a conditional it will usually be symbolized with an existential quantifier. Note that F3 is not an acceptable symbolization of S2.

(F3) $(x)Ex \rightarrow (\exists x)Tx$

F3 represents S3.

(S3)   If everyone passed the exam, someone will throw a party.

In a context such as S2, 'anyone' and 'everyone' cannot be interchanged, but 'anyone' and 'someone' can. S2 and S4 have the same content.

(S4)   If someone passed the exam, someone will throw a party.

A guide to the symbolization of sentences containing 'any' can be based on this observation:

'Any' is symbolized with an existential quantifier iff 'some' can be substituted for 'any' without changing the content of the sentence.

The conjunction S5 may be symbolized by the multiple quantification F5.

(S5) (*Physiologist Knut Schmidt-Nielsen*) "All BIRDS have FEATH-ERS, and all birds have PNEUMATIZED bones."

(F5) (x)(Bx → Fx) & (x)(Bx → Px)

S5 could also be symbolized with a pair of formulas: the two conjuncts of F5. For the sake of uniformity I propose this convention:

One English sentence will be represented by *one* wff.[1]

A second sample conjunction and its symbolization:

(*Dolphin Bill Stanfill*) "Every OFFENSIVE lineman HOLDS, but not every one gets CAUGHT."

(x)(Ox → Hx) & (∃x)(Ox & ~Cx)

Sentences containing the term 'almost all' may be symbolized with conjunctive multiple quantifications; S6 is an example:

(S6) Almost all CARS use GASOLINE.

(F6) (∃x)(Cx & Gx) & (∃x)(Cx & ~Gx)

F6 is logically weaker than S6 (that is, S6 entails F6 but not vice versa), but it is the best symbolization of S6 obtainable in predicate logic.

In section 5.1 I stipulated that a formula is well-formed only if each variable in it lies within the scope of a quantifier containing the same variable. There is a parallel formation principle which we shall also adopt:

A formula is a wff only if no variable in it lies within the scope of two (or more) quantifiers containing the same variable.

By this standard, formula F7 is not a wff because the last two variables (one of which occurs in an existential quantifier) fall within the scope of two quantifiers containing x.

(F7) (x)[Ax → (∃x)Bx]

In punctuating multiple quantifications, care must be taken to avoid violating this principle. F7 may be admitted to the family of wffs simply by omitting the brackets or by substituting another variable (*y* for example) for the last two occurrences of *x*.

---

[1] An exception must be made when both a premise and the conclusion of an argument occur in the same sentence.

8.2
Proofs

The system of rules that we have been employing since Chapter Four is sufficient for constructing proofs for valid arguments involving multiple quantifications. On the whole, these proofs exercise our ingenuity more than did the proofs of earlier chapters. In this section I construct several sample proofs.

Probably the most common type of multiple-quantification argument is one with a conditional conclusion. An example is suggested by the July cartoon in the *1972 Peanuts Datebook*. Lucy announces arrogantly, "If everybody agreed with me—they'd all be right." She could support her statement with this argument:

> If everybody AGREED with Lucy, they'd all be RIGHT—because anyone who agrees with Lucy is right.

The argument symbolized:

$$(x)(Ax \rightarrow Rx) \vdash (x)Ax \rightarrow (x)Rx$$

(UD: people) Since the conclusion is a conditional, the Arrow In strategy may be employed: I make a provisional assumption of the antecedent and attempt to derive the consequent. As the consequent begins with a quantifier, I plan to reach it with the Tilde Out strategy. At this point in my plans I have developed the following proof outline:

(1)	$(x)(Ax \rightarrow Rx)$	A
(2)	$(x)Ax$	PA
(3)	$\sim(x)Rx$	PA
	•	
	•	
	•	
	(standard contradiction)	
	$(x)Rx$	3–? $\sim$O
	$(x)Ax \rightarrow (x)Rx$	2–? $\rightarrow$I

The completed proof:

1	(1)	$(x)(Ax \rightarrow Rx)$	A
2	(2)	$(x)Ax$	PA
3	(3)	$\sim(x)Rx$	PA
3	(4)	$(\exists x)\sim Rx$	3 QE

3	(5)	~Ra	4 EO
1	(6)	Aa → Ra	1 UO
2	(7)	Aa	2 UO
1,2	(8)	Ra	6,7 →O
1,2,3	(9)	Ra & ~Ra	8,5 &I
1,2	(10)	(x)Rx	3–9 ~O
1	(11)	(x)Ax → (x)Rx	2–10 →I

As the proof employs provisional assumptions but is not a standard Tilde proof, the assumption-dependence column must be included. This column is usually needed in proofs which involve multiple quantifications.

The "Lucy" argument can also be validated with a Tilde Out proof. The proof begins:

(1)	(x)(Ax→ Rx)	A
(2)	~ [(x)Ax→ (x)Rx]	PA
(3)	(x)Ax & ~(x)Rx	2 AR

Line 3 is not a universal quantification, and therefore UO cannot be applied to it. It is also not the negation of a quantification, and so QE is not applicable. The next two steps in the proof should be taken with the Ampersand Out Rule:

(4)	(x)Ax	3 &O
(5)	~(x)Rx	3 &O

The remainder of the proof is straightforward. The completed proof will be one line longer than the Arrow In proof of the previous paragraph, but (being a standard Tilde proof) it avoids the assumption-dependence column.

Some arguments involving multiple quantifications have conditional *premises*, for example:

> If even one child is ROWDY, every child will go to DETENTION. Hence, any rowdy child will have detention.

Symbolized:

$$(\exists x)Rx \rightarrow (x)Dx \vdash (x)(Rx \rightarrow Dx)$$

(UD: children in the class) I begin the proof with the Tilde Out strategy:

(1)	(∃x)Rx → (x)Dx	A
(2)	~(x)(Rx → Dx)	PA

I cannot apply EO or UO to the wff on line 1, since it is neither an existential nor a universal quantification. Line 1 is a conditional and it can be treated with the Arrow Out Rule if the appropriate second premise ('$(\exists x)Rx$') is provided. This suggests two possible strategies for the proof:

(a) Make a provisional assumption of '$(\exists x)Rx$', apply the Arrow Out Rule to line 1 and the provisional assumption, and eliminate the provisional assumption later in the proof by a step of Tilde In.

(b) Make a provisional assumption of '$\sim(\exists x)Rx$', reach a standard contradiction, derive '$(\exists x)Rx$' by Tilde Out, and finally make the Arrow Out step.

Line 1 may also be treated with the Modus Tollens Rule if the proper second premise ('$\sim(x)Dx$') is supplied. So there are two more strategies which parallel (a) and (b). I illustrate strategy (a):

1	(1)	$(\exists x)Rx \rightarrow (x)Dx$	A
2	(2)	$\sim(x)(Rx \rightarrow Dx)$	PA
3	(3)	$(\exists x)Rx$	PA
1,3	(4)	$(x)Dx$	1,3 $\rightarrow$O
2	(5)	$(\exists x)\sim(Rx \rightarrow Dx)$	2 QE
2	(6)	$\sim(Ra \rightarrow Da)$	5 EO
1,3	(7)	Da	4 UO
2	(8)	$Ra \& \sim Da$	6 AR
2	(9)	$\sim Da$	8 &O
1,2,3	(10)	$Da \& \sim Da$	7,9 &I

Having reached a standard contradiction I will be able to eliminate the provisional assumption on line 3. Then I shall aim for a second standard contradiction so that the remaining provisional assumption (line 2) can be dropped.

1,2	(11)	$\sim(\exists x)Rx$	3–10 $\sim$I
1,2	(12)	$(x)\sim Rx$	11 QE
1,2	(13)	$\sim Ra$	12 UO
2	(14)	Ra	8 &O
1,2	(15)	$Ra \& \sim Ra$	14,13 &I
1	(16)	$(x)(Rx \rightarrow Dx)$	2–15 $\sim$O

A proof for the same argument employing strategy (b) (see the previous paragraph):

1	(1)	$(\exists x)Rx \rightarrow (x)Dx$	A .
2	(2)	$\sim(x)(Rx \rightarrow Dx)$	PA

3	(3)	~(∃x)Rx	PA
2	(4)	(∃x)~(Rx → Dx)	2 QE
3	(5)	(x)~Rx	3 QE
2	(6)	~(Ra → Da)	4 EO
3	(7)	~Ra	5 UO
2	(8)	Ra & ~Da	6 AR
2	(9)	Ra	8 &O
2,3	(10)	Ra & ~Ra	9,7 &I

Having reached a standard contradiction, I am able to eliminate the provisional assumption on line 3, reaching a wff (on line 11) which matches the antecedent of line 1 thereby setting up an Arrow Out step. The proof continues:

2	(11)	(∃x)Rx	3-10 ~O
1,2	(12)	(x)Dx	1,11 →O
1,2	(13)	Da	12 UO
2	(14)	~Da	8 &O
1,2	(15)	Da & ~Da	13,14 &I
1	(16)	(x)(Rx → Dx)	2-15 ~O

Ordinarily any one of the four strategies mentioned above (two Arrow Out and two Modus Tollens strategies) may be used in proofs of arguments with multiply quantified conditional premises. For a given proof, some of the strategies may be more economical than the others.

Some predicate arguments have conjunctive premises or conclusions, but these present no problems. Conjunctive premises are "broken up" by applications of the Ampersand Out Rule and conjunctive conclusions are reached by Ampersand In.

Arguments with disjunctive conclusions may be proven with the *Tilde Out — DeMorgan's Law strategy*. A provisional assumption is made of the negation of the conclusion; this assumption is then transformed into a conjunction by application of DeMorgan's Law. Arguments with disjunctive premises are not handled so neatly. A sample argument with a disjunctive premise:

> Either all of Smudgie's kittens are MALES or all are FEMALES [since they are anatomically identical]. Some of them must be females [because they are calicoes]. No female kittens are male. Therefore, all the kittens are female.

The argument symbolized:

(x)Mx ∨ (x)Fx, (∃x)Fx, (x)(Fx → ~Mx) ⊢ (x)Fx

(UD: Smudgie's kittens) There are at least two proof strategies open to us. We could construct a Wedge Out proof, making a provisional assumption of the left disjunct of the first premise and then later in the proof a provisional assumption of the right disjunct. A second plan is suggested by the fact that the conclusion matches one of the disjuncts of the first premise. The idea is to derive the negation of the other disjunct so that the proof can be completed with a step of Disjunctive Argument. As Wedge Out proofs are tedious, I opt for the latter strategy.

1	(1)	(x)Mx ∨ (x)Fx	A	[1]
2	(2)	(∃x)Fx	A	[2]
3	(3)	(x)(Fx → ~Mx)	A	[3]
4	(4)	(x)Mx	PA	[6]
2	(5)	Fa	2 EO	[7]
3	(6)	Fa → ~Ma	3 UO	[8]
4	(7)	Ma	4 UO	[9]
2,3	(8)	~Ma	6,5 →O	[10]
2,3,4	(9)	Ma & ~Ma	7,8 &I	[11]
2,3	(10)	~(x)Mx	4–9 ~I	[5]
1,2,3	(11)	(x)Fx	1,10 DA	[4]

Bracketed numerals indicate the order of proof discovery. By now it should be clear that UO cannot be applied to line 1. This is not a standard Tilde proof because the last line is not reached by a Tilde Rule; hence, the assumption-dependence column is needed.

Occasionally in a proof for a multiple-quantification argument it will be necessary to apply UO or EO *twice* to one line. There are proofs of this sort in challenge exercises for this chapter.

The following table reveals interesting patterns involving the quantifiers, the ampersand, and the wedge:

(F1)	(∃x)(Ax & Bx)	F1 entails F2
(F2)	(∃x)Ax & (∃x)Bx	but not vice versa.
(F3)	(∃x)(Ax ∨ Bx)	F3 and F4 are
(F4)	(∃x)Ax ∨ (∃x)Bx	logically equivalent.
(F5)	(x)(Ax & Bx)	F5 and F6 are
(F6)	(x)Ax & (x)Bx	logically equivalent.
(F7)	(x)(Ax ∨ Bx)	F8 entails F7
(F8)	(x)Ax ∨ (x)Bx	but not vice versa.

These results are the subject of exercises 64 and 214 (Chapter Eight), and exercises 81 and 82 (Chapter Nine).

EXERCISES

60. Symbolize these statements with multiple quantifications.

   (a) *(Headline)* "Some STORES will take back PANTYHOSE and some won't."

   *(b) *(Philosopher Ernest Nagel)* ". . . If there are no UNICORNS, then all unicorns are BLACK."

   (c) *(Mark Twain)* "Everybody TALKS about the weather, but nobody DOES anything about it." (UD: people; $Dx = x$ does something about the weather)

   (d) *(Justice Frankfurter)* "If one man is allowed to DETERMINE for himself what is law, every man can." (UD: people)

   (e) *(Philosopher R. E. Hobart)* "All compulsion is causation, but not all causation is compulsion." ($Ax = x$ is an instance of compulsion, $Bx = x$ is an instance of causation)

   (f) Either one of the CHILDREN is AWAKE or there is an INTRUDER.

   *(g) *(Newspaper)* "If any member of the [auto] INDUSTRY can MEET the [clean air] act's deadlines, any APPLICATIONS for a delay will be DENIED."

   (h) *(Magazine ad)* "Only Coke is Coca-Cola and only Coca-Cola is Coke." ($Ax = x$ is Coke,[2] $Bx = x$ is Coca-Cola[2])

   (i) *(Basketball player Bob Lanier)* "If anyone is SUSPENDED or FINED, all the players will QUIT." (UD: NBA players)

   (j) *(Novel)* "Not all COPS and not all PRIESTS are [expletive deleted]." ($Mx = x$ is a [expletive deleted])

   (k) *(Bumper sticker)* "If GUNS were OUTLAWED only outlaws would have guns." ($Ax = x$ is an outlaw, $Bx = x$ has a gun)

   (l) *(Children's book)* "Some people SCREAMED, some people RAN, and some people did both." (UD: people)

   (m) *(TV commercial)* "Klean & Shine CLEANS almost everything in your house." (UD: household articles; $Cx =$ Klean & Shine[2] cleans x)

   *(n) *(Philosophy book)* "Only some SPIRITS ENJOY this vision."

61. Translate each wff into a colloquial English sentence using the dictionary provided.

   $Mx = x$ is mental
   $Px = x$ is physical

   (a) $(\exists x)Mx$ & $(\exists x)Px$

   (b) $(x)Px \lor (\exists x)Mx$

   [2] Registered trade-mark.

°(c) (∃x)~Px → (∃x)Mx

(d) (x)Px → (x)~Mx

(e) (∃x)(Px & Mx) → (x)(Mx → Px)

62. Complete the following proofs (including assumption-dependence columns). Every assumption has been identified.

°(a) 1   (1)   (x)(Ax → Bx)   A

           (2)   PA

           (3)   PA

           (4)   2 EO

           (5)   1 UO

           (6)   3 UO

           (7)   5,6 →O

           (8)   7,4 &I

           (9)   3–8 ~I

           (10)   (∃x)~Bx → ~(x)Ax   2–9 →I

(b) 1   (1)   (∃x)Ax → (x)~Bx   A

           (2)   ~(x)(Bx → ~Ax)   PA

           (3)   (∃x)~(Bx → ~Ax)

           (4)   (∃x)Ax   PA

           (5)   (x)~Bx

           (6)   ~(Ba → ~Aa)

           (7)   ~Ba

           (8)   Ba & ~~Aa

           (9)   Ba

           (10)   Ba & ~Ba

           (11)   ~(∃x)Ax

           (12)   (x)~Ax

           (13)   ~Aa

           (14)   ~~Aa

           (15)   ~Aa & ~~Aa

           (16)   (x)(Bx → ~Ax)

Instructions for exercises 63 through 71: Symbolize the arguments and construct proofs for them. All are valid.

63. A guest on the "Phil Donahue Show" said (paraphrased):

> *Only SINNERS NEED churches. If there were no sinners, no one would need a church.*

Show that the first sentence entails the second.

*64. In a day when the government exerts pressure on colleges to hire teachers from the various minority categories, a person who represents more than one minority or disadvantaged group is an administrator's delight. The following argument expresses this theme:

> There is a LATIN WOMAN in the department. So, we have a Latin in our department and we have a woman.

(UD: people in the department)

65. In the second panel of the "Conchy" comic strip, the rooster states a proverb, and in the fourth panel he supports it.

> If a COCK crows at NIGHT, someone will DIE, because any cock who crows at night will die [at the hands of humans].

The term 'someone' in the conclusion must be understood to apply to animals as well as humans.

April 3, 1974. CONCHY by Jim Childress, courtesy of Field Newspaper Syndicate.

66. None of the employees attending the PICNIC was BLACK. Consequently, either some employees did not attend or none of the employees is black.

(UD: employees)

*67. A sports story reports an interview with Patriot quarterback Jim Plunkett after a defeat in which Patriot receivers dropped five passes.

> *Someone mentioned that if Plunkett had decided not to throw to a receiver who dropped a pass, he wouldn't have had anyone at which to throw. Plunkett just laughed.*[3]

An argument lurks behind this remark:

> Every receiver DROPPED passes. Therefore, if Plunkett THROWS to no receiver who dropped a pass, he doesn't have anyone at which to throw.

(UD: Plunkett's receivers)

[3]Al Levine, "Patriot Fans Voice Disapproval," *Miami News*, December 4, 1972, p. 6-C.

68. The editors of an American literature text offer this scholium on the thirteenth paragraph of Emerson's "Divinity School Address":

Jesus Christ was God incarnate; the divine Jesus was also man; therefore another man, by being true to the God incarnate in him, may also be "divine" in the sense that Jesus was.[4]

A formalization of this argument:

<u>Jesus</u> was DIVINE and a MAN. If any man was divine, then all men are divine. It follows that all men are divine.

69. *Time* describes an experimental sixth-grade class in philosophy and logic. When the teacher (see below) asked the class, "What would it be like if all animals were cats?" a girl replied, "Elephants would have whiskers." This argument represents the student's inference:

CATS have WHISKERS. ELEPHANTS are ANIMALS. So, if all animals were cats, elephants would have whiskers.

Sixth-grade philosophy class in Newark
Photo by Ted Thai. Time Magazine. ©
Time, Inc.

[4]Sculley Bradley, Richmond Croom Beatty, E. Hudson Long, and George Perkins, eds., *The American Tradition in Literature* (4th ed.; New York: Grosset & Dunlap, 1974), I, 1097, n. 1.

70. A news story quotes the following statement made by a black sociologist:

"If you define nigger as someone whose life-style is defined by others, whose opportunities are defined by others, whose role in society is defined by others, then, good news! You don't have to be black to be a nigger in this society. Most of the people in America are niggers."

The sociologist's argument:

Many non-BLACKS have a LIFE-style which is determined by others. Hence, if "NIGGER" is defined as "one whose life-style is determined by others," then not all "niggers" are black.

(UD: Americans)

71. Prove that Flo Capp's statement S1 entails S2.

  (S1) "A good lookin' one could do better, an' a sensible one would know better!"

  (S2) A woman who is either good LOOKING or SENSIBLE either could DO better than Andy or would KNOW better than to take up with Andy.

(UD: women)

December 10, 1973. © 1973 Daily Mirror Newspapers Ltd. ANDY CAPP by Reggie Smythe. Courtesy Field Newspaper Syndicate.

214. (CHALLENGING) This table was presented at the end of section 8.2.

(F1)	(∃x)(Ax & Bx)	F1 entails F2
(F2)	(∃x)Ax & (∃x)Bx	but not vice versa.
(F3)	(∃x)(Ax ∨ Bx)	F3 and F4 are
(F4)	(∃x)Ax ∨ (∃x)Bx	logically equivalent.
(F5)	(x)(Ax & Bx)	F5 and F6 are
(F6)	(x)Ax & (x)Bx	logically equivalent.
(F7)	(x)(Ax ∨ Bx)	F8 entails F7
(F8)	(x)Ax ∨ (x)Bx	but not vice versa.

In working exercise 64 you showed (in effect) that F1 entails F2. Now establish by formal proof that:

  (a) F3 entails F4.

(b) F4 entails F3.

(c) F5 entails F6.

(d) F6 entails F5.

(e) F8 entails F7.

Demonstrate by diagram that F2 does not entail F1. Does the diagram method (as explained in Chapter Six) establish that F7 does not entail F8? Explain.

215. (CHALLENGING) This table reveals unexpected patterns involving the quantifiers and the arrow. Each wff entails all the wffs beneath it. F5 and F6 are logically equivalent. No wff entails any wff above it. F3 does not entail F4, and F4 does not entail F3.

$$(F1) \quad (\exists x)Ax \to (x)Bx$$
$$(F2) \quad (x)(Ax \to Bx)$$

(F3) (x)Ax → (x)Bx	(F4) (∃x)Ax → (∃x)Bx
(F5) (x)Ax → (∃x)Bx	(F6) (∃x)(Ax → Bx)

The "detention" argument of section 8.2 parallels F1's entailment of F2, and the "Lucy" argument in the same section amounts to F2's entailment of F3. Exercise 65 concerned F2's entailment of F4. Establish by formal proof that:

(a) F3 entails F5.

(b) F4 entails F6.

(c) F5 entails F6.

(d) F6 entails F5.

216. (CHALLENGING) F1 is the literal symbolization of S1.

(S1) If some person has the right to PUNISH, then all people have that right.

(F1) (∃x)Px → (x)Px

(F2) (x)(y)(Px ↔ Py)

(UD: people) F2 is an acceptable alternative symbolization of S1 iff F1 and F2 are logically equivalent. Establish their equivalence by constructing two formal proofs. Incidentally, F2 is not equivalent to F3. This shows once again the importance of quantifier scope.

(F3) (x)Px ↔ (y)Py

F3 is a logical truth. Establish this by constructing a proof in which F3 is derived *free of assumptions*.

chapter nine

Interpretations

9.1
Introduction

The diagram technique explained in Chapter Six can be applied to a large number of predicate arguments, but there are many predicate arguments to which it is inapplicable. These include arguments involving relations, multiple quantifications, or more than four predicates.[1] In dealing with such arguments we must turn to other logical techniques. The method of formal proofs will establish the validity of *any* valid predicate argument (which can be symbolized in the notation of this book). The purpose of the present chapter is to present a logical technique — called "the method of interpretation"[2] — which can be used to demonstrate the invalidity of *any* invalid predicate argument. (In fact, the scope of the method is broader than this; it is applicable to any invalid argument belonging to any branch of deductive logic!) I introduce the technique in this section, and in section 9.2 I show how it is applied to mul-

---

[1] The diagram technique *as set out in Chapter Six* treats only arguments having fewer than five predicates. Diagrams can be devised for arguments with more predicates, but they are cumbersome.

[2] The method of interpretation is also called the "method of counterexample" and the "method of negative demonstration."

tiply-quantified arguments. In section 11.2 the method will be extended to relational arguments.

The method of interpretation is a formal version of a very old logical device which I call the "method of refutation by logical analogy." The latter method is employed by Fran in this dialogue:

> STEVE: "GOOD philosophical papers are always ARGUMENTA-
> TIVE. My paper on Plato is argumentative. So, it must be a
> good philosophical paper."
>
> FRAN: "Wait a minute. That's like arguing: 'Cats are always mam-
> mals. Flipper is a mammal. So, Flipper must be a cat.'"

Fran refutes Steve's argument by inventing an analogous argument that is obviously invalid. The two arguments are analogous because they exhibit the same logical form. Since they have the same logical form and the "Flipper" argument is invalid, the "Plato" argument must also be invalid. Fran's analogy is obviously invalid because its premises are known to be true and its conclusion is clearly false. By the definition of *validity*, a valid argument cannot have (all) true premises and a false conclusion.

I will apply the method of interpretation to Steve's "Plato" argument. The similarity between this technique and the method of refutation by logical analogy will be apparent. First we symbolize the argument whose invalidity is to be demonstrated:

$$(x)(Gx \to Ax), \ Ap \vdash Gp$$

(UD: philosophical papers) The symbols which occur in the wffs of predicate logic may be divided into two classes: *logical* and *descriptive* symbols. The logical symbols are variables, quantifiers, groupers, and statement connectives; the descriptive symbols are predicate letters and names. The meanings of the logical symbols remain constant; the descriptive symbols, on the other hand, abbreviate different expressions in different problems. In the symbolized argument above, G abbreviates the predicate 'is good', but in other symbolizations it will abbreviate other predicates. If we assign new expressions to the descriptive symbols occurring in Steve's argument, the result will be a second argument which has the *same form* as Steve's argument but *different content*. An example:

> $Gx = x$ is a cat
>
> $Ax = x$ is a mammal
>
> $p = $ Flipper

All that remains to be done is to specify a new UD: animals. The resulting argument is, of course, Fran's argument:

All cats are mammals.   *(True)*

Flipper is a mammal.   *(True)*

So, Flipper is a cat.   *(False)*

Because this argument has true premises and a false conclusion, it must be invalid. The "Flipper" and "Plato" arguments have the same symbolization, and therefore the same logical form. Since invalidity is a matter of form, the "Plato" argument must also be invalid.

Selecting an expression to be abbreviated by a descriptive symbol is known to logicians as "interpreting" the symbol. The argument which results from interpreting all the descriptive symbols in a symbolized argument (and specifying a UD) is called an "interpretation." A recipe for employing the method of interpretation:

(1) **Symbolize the argument to be tested.**
(2) **Specify a UD.**
(3) **Interpret each descriptive symbol. (Predicate letters are interpreted with predicates and names with singular terms.)**
(4) **Formulate the reinterpreted argument in English, and note the truth value of each premise and the conclusion.**

If each premise of the reinterpreted argument is known (by you) to be true and the conclusion is known to be false, then the original argument has been proven invalid.

Since the method of interpretation is so similar to the informal technique of refutation by logical analogy, some may view the latter simpler technique as the preferable method. If your aim is to convince someone with no logical training of the invalidity of an argument, then the informal approach is ideal. But if your goal is to establish invalidity to your own satisfaction and to the satisfaction of others with knowledge of logic, then the method of interpretation is generally preferable — first, because this method if properly employed guarantees that the original argument and the analogical one have the same form (assuming that the symbolization was adequate), and second, because using the method can help you invent the analogical argument.

I further illustrate the technique by testing several arguments. The philosopher A. C. Ewing criticizes the view that the phenomenon of understanding is completely explainable in terms of sensory images. He writes:

> *In any case, as I have said, in e.g. philosophy and economics (or even politics) the meaning of most statements cannot possibly be expressed in terms of sensuous imagery which is like the subject-matter of our thought. Yet we can understand some statements in philosophy and economics. Therefore understanding is something mental which cannot possibly be explained entirely in terms of images.*[3]

[3]A. C. Ewing, *The Fundamental Questions of Philosophy* (New York: The Crowell-Collier Publishing Company, 1962), p. 114.

If we drop the reference to economics for the sake of simplicity, we may formalize part of Ewing's argument as a syllogism:

> Some PHILOSOPHICAL statements do not evoke IMAGERY. We can UNDERSTAND some statements in philosophy. Therefore, some understandable statements do not evoke imagery.

Symbolized:

$$(\exists x)(Px \ \& \ {\sim}Ix), (\exists x)(Ux \ \& \ Px) \vdash (\exists x)(Ux \ \& \ {\sim}Ix)$$

(UD: statements) Ewing's argument is invalid, as this interpretation reveals:

> UD: people
>
> $Px = x$ is an American
> $Ix = x$ is a Protestant
> $Ux = x$ is a Lutheran

> Some Americans are not Protestants.   (T)
>
> Some Lutherans are Americans.   (T)
>
> Therefore, some Lutherans are not Protestants.   (F)

Consider this invalid argument:

> Any drug PUSHER who is RESPONSIBLE for his actions is WICKED. No drug ADDICT is responsible for his acts. Thus, every non-addicted pusher is wicked.

The argument symbolized:

$$(x)[(Px \ \& \ Rx) \rightarrow Wx], (x)(Ax \rightarrow {\sim}Rx) \vdash (x)[({\sim}Ax \ \& \ Px) \rightarrow Wx]$$

An interpretation which establishes invalidity:

> UD: people
>
> $Px = x$ is male
> $Rx = x$ is a parent
> $Wx = x$ is a father
> $Ax = x$ is an infant

> All male parents are fathers.   (T)
>
> No infants are parents.   (T)
>
> So, every noninfant male is a father.   (F)

Many logicians favor arithmetical interpretations. One advantage of such interpretations is that the resulting statements are *necessarily* true or *necessarily* false. Logicians like to achieve results that hold with necessity. A second advantage of these interpretations is that the truth values of (simple) arithmetical statements can be calculated easily and quickly. There is no need to refer to encyclopedias and the like. A sample arithmetical interpretation of the "pusher" argument:

UD: integers[4]

Px = x is odd
Rx = x is greater than 3
Wx = x is greater than 4
Ax = x is less than 3

Any odd integer greater than 3 is greater than 4.   (T)

No integer less than 3 is greater than 3.   (T)

Any integer not less than 3 which is odd is greater than 4.   (F)

The number 3 itself accounts for the falsity of the conclusion: it is not less than 3 and it is odd, but it is not greater than 4.

The customary method of specifying a UD is to name a class, such as *people, Lutherans, integers*. A second acceptable way of stipulating a UD is to name all the members of a class. The following notations specify the same UD:

UD: prime numbers less than 6

UD: {1, 2, 3, 5}

Braces are employed in the second notation to mark the difference between stipulating a class by name and doing it by listing its members.

Exercise 56 (Chapter Seven) concerns this penevalid (thus invalid) argument:

All CONIFERS are PINES. Hence, some conifers are pines.

(x)(Cx → Px) ⊢ (∃x)(Cx & Px)

Any successful interpretation of the argument will have the predicate letter C denoting a property which is *not* possessed by any member of the stated UD. For example:

UD: {1}

Cx = x is even
Px = x is even

All even integers are even.   (T)

So, some even integers are even.   (F)

The conclusion is false, since it claims the existence of an even number in the set whose sole member is odd. As this example illustrates, two (or more) predicate letters may be given the same interpretation. (Also, when a symbolized argument is reinterpreted, a given descriptive symbol may retain its initial interpretation.)

An A statement (or an E) whose grammatical subject denotes nothing

---

[4] By 'integers' I mean the natural numbers (as one, two, and so on), their negatives, and zero.

is *vacuously true*. Thus, if the UD consists exclusively of odd integers, S1 is true.

(S1) All even integers are primes.

Why this should be so becomes clearer when we reformulate S1 as S2.

(S2) There are no even integers that aren't primes.

If the UD contains no even integers, *period,* then it contains none that aren't primes. Sometimes one can make good use of *vacuous truths* in devising interpretations.

Some tips on inventing interpretations: Select a UD which may be divided into commonly recognized subclasses. My favorite UD's (all of which have been used in this section) are integers, animals, and people. One useful way of subdividing the class of people is along religious lines (*Catholics, Protestants, Methodists,* and so on). Devise interpretations for the descriptive symbols appearing in the conclusion of the argument which make the conclusion false. Generally, this will be easy to do. Then interpret the remaining descriptive symbol(s) in a way that makes the premise(s) true. Often, this step requires ingenuity. Sometimes you will discover that your interpretation of the conclusion makes a true interpretation of the premises impossible; in this case you must begin again. Your ability to devise successful interpretations will improve with practice.

The statements composing the newly devised argument should deal with subject matters of common knowledge so that their truth values will be known to others who may examine your work. For example, S3 is acceptable (in the United States in the 1970s) but S4 is not.

(S3) Some of Gerald Ford's children are female.

(S4) Some of Millard Fillmore's children are female.

There are three logical restrictions on the technique of interpretation:

(1) The UD must have at least one member.

(2) Names must be interpreted with singular terms (not predicates), and each singular term must denote a member of the UD.

(3) Predicate letters must be interpreted with predicates (not singular terms).

As noted earlier in the section, a predicate used in an interpretation may denote a property that is possessed by no member of the UD.

With the help of the concept of "interpretation" we can give this definition of *validity* for predicate arguments:

A predicate argument is valid iff it is impossible to devise an interpretation with all true premises and a false conclusion.

Notice, however, that failing to devise such an interpretation does not demonstrate the validity of an argument. Failing to invent an interpretation with true premises and false conclusion does not show that it is *impossible* to devise one. However, when a person who is skilled in the technique fails to construct such an interpretation after many attempts, he is justified in *suspecting* that the argument under investigation is valid.

9.2
Multiple Quantification

If we transpose the premise and the conclusion of the "Lucy" argument of Chapter Eight, we reach this invalid multiply-quantified argument:

> If everybody AGREED with Lucy, they'd all be RIGHT. Therefore, anyone who agrees with Lucy is right.

The argument resists treatment by diagrams, for we have no way of diagraming its conditional premise. The method of interpretation handles the argument easily:

$(x)Ax \rightarrow (x)Rx \vdash (x)(Ax \rightarrow Rx)$

UD: people

$Ax = x$ is male
$Rx = x$ is wifeless

> If everyone is male, then everyone is wifeless.   (T)

> Therefore, every male is wifeless.   (F)

A second interpretation which, while less ingenious and less intuitive, proves invalidity just as conclusively:

UD: $\{1, 2\}$

$Ax = x$ is even
$Rx = x$ is greater than 2

> If every integer is even, then every integer is greater than 2.   (T)

> Therefore, every even integer is greater than 2.   (F)

Not every integer in the set $\{1, 2\}$ is even; hence, the antecedent of the premise is false. So, the premise is true, because a conditional with a false antecedent is true.

In constructing interpretations for multiply-quantified arguments it is useful to remember these principles of propositional logic:

> **A conjunction is true iff each conjunct is true.**

> **A disjunction is false iff each disjunct is false.**

> **A conditional is false iff its antecedent is true and its consequent is false.**

> **A biconditional is true iff its two components have the same truth value.**

A radio newscaster (WIOD) jazzed up his weather report with this statement:

> *If seeing is believing, there are no believers in Dade County this morning — the area is covered with fog.*

Presumably he viewed the following as a valid inference:

> There are no SEERS in Dade County this morning. Consequently, if all seers are BELIEVERS, then there are no believers in Dade County this morning.

Symbolized:

$$\sim(\exists x)Sx \vdash (x)(Sx \to Bx) \to \sim(\exists x)Bx$$

(UD: Dade Countians on the morning of January 24, 1972) An interpretation which demonstrates the invalidity of this argument:

> UD: dogs
>
> $Sx = x$ is a cat
> $Bx = x$ is a mammal
>
> There are no cats. (T)
> If all cats are mammals, then there are no mammals. (F)

The premise is true for a UD of dogs. The antecedent of the conclusion is vacuously true and the consequent is false; so, the conclusion is false.

EXERCISES

Instructions for exercises 72 through 82: Establish the invalidity of each argument by the method of interpretation. (1) Symbolize the argument; (2) specify a UD; (3) interpret the descriptive symbols; and (4) formulate the reinterpreted argument in English, noting truth values.

72. Jacques Cousteau writes:

> *Some years ago, it seems, a European aquarium ran short of sea water just as it received a shipment of live salt water fish.*
>
> *Since the formula for sea water is well known, the curators decided to manufacture some. This was soon done. But when a fish was released in it, it died.*
>
> *Then, an inspiration! Just the tiniest drop of real sea water was added to a tub full of the man-made — and the fish that were put in it lived!*
>
> *Is this not marvelous? It implies that each of the trillions of drops that comprise the great oceans has a life of its own, an invisible spark that we do not understand, but that makes possible the incredible myriads of marine life forms.*[5]

[5] From a form letter written for the Cousteau Society, Inc., April, 1974, p. 1.

The passage suggests this argument:

> The <u>drop</u> of ocean water added to the tub by the curators was LIFE-sustaining. This implies that each drop of ocean water is life-sustaining.

(UD: drops of ocean water) "Drops of ocean water" is the UD to be used in symbolizing the Cousteau argument; it need not be the UD employed in the reinterpretation.

73. Lee Trevino, upon winning the British Open:

> *I had never won a championship on this side of the water and I believe that a really world class golfer must pick up titles in countries outside the United States. I think that now I must be regarded as world class.*[6]

Trevino may have been reasoning:

> A WORLD class golfer must win championships OUTSIDE the United States. Therefore, since I have won a championship outside the United States, I am a world class golfer.

(UD: golfers; $t =$ Trevino)

*74. The philosophers John Burr and Milton Goldinger (claiming to summarize a piece by Bertrand Russell) write:

> *All causes differ from their effects because otherwise all causes would be identical with their effects.*[7]

This argument formalized:

> It is false that all CAUSES are IDENTICAL with their effects. So, no causes are identical with their effects.

($Ix = x$ is identical with its effect)

75. Flo Capp appears to draw this inference:

> <u>Andy</u> is a PERSON. Andy is HOPELESS. Hence, all people are hopeless.

June 10, 1971. © 1971 Daily Mirror Newspapers Ltd. ANDY CAPP by Reggie Smythe. Courtesy Field Newspaper Syndicate.

[6] "Trevino Calls Himself a 2nd Cassius Clay," *Miami News*, July 12, 1971, p. 3-B.

[7] John R. Burr and Milton Goldinger (eds.), *Philosophy and Contemporary Issues* (New York: The Macmillan Company, 1972), p. 317.

76. When the Scarecrow begs the Wizard of Oz for brains, the Wizard replies:

    You don't need them. You are learning something every day. A baby has brains, but it doesn't know much. . . .[8]

    This response suggests an argument:

    BABIES HAVE brains. Babies do not KNOW much. Thus, it is false that having brains is a necessary condition for knowing a lot.

    ($Hx = x$ has brains, $Kx = x$ knows much) The conclusion entails that some individuals know much and also that some individuals lack brains, while the premise set has neither entailment. In order that the argument not be invalidated on this trivial ground, include the following existential premises:

    Some individuals know much. Some individuals lack brains.

*77. Dear Abby advises "Hurt in Alabama":

    A man who wears a wedding ring obviously doesn't mind announcing to the world that he's married, but it doesn't necessarily follow that the married man who wears no ring is reluctant to admit it.[9]

    Support Abby's claim that the second statement does not follow from the first. (UD: men; $Rx = x$ wears a wedding ring, $Ax = x$ is willing to admit that he is married, $Mx = x$ is married)

78. This conversation took place at spring registration:

    UNDERGRADUATE: *"Who is an advisor?"*

    POSPESEL: *"Anyone wearing a TIE is an ADVISOR."*

    MCGRAW: *"But I'm an advisor and I'm not wearing a tie."*

    (UD: people; m = McGraw) Ms. McGraw believed that her comment entailed the denial of my claim. Show that she was mistaken.

79. In a column on the proposed Constitutional amendment sanctioning school prayer, William Buckley writes:

    Well, the bishops' representative said, if the Constitution authorizes nondenominational prayer, then doesn't it indirectly forbid denominational prayer?[10]

    Buckley suggests that the bishops' representative viewed this inference as valid:

    All nondenominational prayers are PERMITTED. Hence, no DENOMINATIONAL prayers are permitted.

    (UD: prayers)

[8] L. Frank Baum, *The Wizard of Oz* (N.p.: The Reilly & Lee Co., 1956), p. 180.

[9] Abigail Van Buren, "Dear Abby" (Chicago Tribune-New York News Syndicate, Inc.), *Miami News,* February 22, 1974, p. 2-C.

[10] "Church Fusses, Misses the Point," *Miami Herald,* November 7, 1971, p. 2-L.

80. I once examined a manuscript for a logic text which contained this passage:

    A SOUND argument, then, is a VALID argument whose premises are TRUE. It follows that an unsound argument is a valid argument with at least one false premise.

    (UD: arguments; $Tx =$ all of x's premises are true) These sentences are *definitions.* The passage establishes (what no one doubted anyway) that logicians sometimes reason erroneously.

81. Argument 64 (Chapter Eight) "stood on its head":

    We have a LATIN in our department and we have a WOMAN. So, there is a Latin woman in the department.

    (UD: people in the department)

*82. A terrorist is either STUPID or WICKED Therefore, either all terrorists are stupid or all of them are wicked.

    (UD: terrorists) Would this argument be valid if the premise and conclusion were interchanged?

217. (CHALLENGING) A televiewer wrote a letter to the CBS program "60 Minutes" in which he claimed that Morley Safer lacked class because he had mispronounced some word. Safer replied on the show (paraphrased):

    If anyone has CLASS, Walter Cronkite does. He MISPRONOUNCES some words ['February', for example]. So, it is false that people who mispronounce words necessarily lack class.

    (UD: people) Using the method of interpretation demonstrate the invalidity of Safer's argument. Add an obviously true premise which converts the argument into a valid one. Construct a formal proof for the modified argument.

218. (CHALLENGING) The following table was presented in Exercise 215 (Chapter Eight):

$$(F1) \quad (\exists x)Ax \to (x)Bx$$
$$(F2) \quad (x)(Ax \to Bx)$$

(F3)	$(x)Ax \to (x)Bx$	(F4)	$(\exists x)Ax \to (\exists x)Bx$
(F5)	$(x)Ax \to (\exists x)Bx$	(F6)	$(\exists x)(Ax \to Bx)$

It was claimed in that exercise that no wff in this table entails any wff above it, that F3 does not entail F4, and that F4 does not entail F3. I showed in Section 9.2 that F3 does not entail F2. Establish by interpretation that:

(a) F2 doesn't entail F1.

(b) F4 doesn't entail F2.

(c) F3 doesn't entail F4.

(d) F4 doesn't entail F3.

(e) F5 doesn't entail F3.

(f) F6 doesn't entail F4.

Optional: Use the same interpretation of A and B in all six problems. (Several UD's will be required.)

219. (CHALLENGING) In Exercise 208 (Chapter Five) I claimed that F1 and F4 are not logically equivalent.

(F1) (x)(Fx → Ga)

(F4) (x)Fx → Ga

If either wff entails the other, show this by formal proof; if either wff fails to entail the other, demonstrate this by interpretation. In Exercise 208 I also claim the nonequivalence of F2 and F3.

(F2) (∃x)Fx → Ga

(F3) (∃x)(Fx → Ga)

Use formal proofs and/or interpretations to determine whether either wff entails the other.

220. (CHALLENGING) Solve the puzzle.

Quine's Dream

ACROSS	DOWN

ACROSS

1. A UD is one.
6. Provides criteria of validity
11. None but
12. Troubled isle
14. Direction
16. Patriotic Mss.
17. (x)
18. Quantifier rule
19. Fib
21. Twelfth letter for logic's father
22. Seymour (dim.)
23. Select one for an interpretation.
24. Gallic copula
26. PAUL or TED is absent.
28. Cliff
29. Men oft attacked
31. Do this to diagram '(x)Fx'.
32. A successful interpretation has a ___ conclusion.
33. A ___ cannot establish invalidity.
37. Truth entails only ___.
42. King, of Avon's bard
43. Symbolization simplifiers
45. Black netter
46. Bug
47. Tilde rule
48. Ampersand cum tilde rule
50. Ms. with a habit
51. *E* adjective
52. Grass
53. Sooner learning site
55. Palmetto state (abbr.)
56. Opthalmic fluid
57. '___valid' means nearly valid.
59. 17a
60. Rabbis ___ if some rabbis are Japanese.

DOWN

2. Behold!
3. Conjunction
4. Card contract
5. Sweet liquid
6. A UD has at ___ one member.
7. European airport
8. Dodger great, Hodges
9. Arrow ___ reduces assumptions.
10. UO and EO
13. Connective
15. 1800 P.M.
18. Campus enclosure
20. To apply EO to part of a line
23. Famous Irish coach
25. Universal statements
27. '(x)Fx $\vdash$ ($\exists$x)Fx' is ___.
28. Arrow rule
30. 'Fx' isn't one.
31. 1a
33. Wise proof-makers start with them.
34. Tahoe town
35. Cereal
36. Disjunction
38. Heyerdahl's bark
39. Floating service
40. Ergo
41. 40d
43. '($\exists$x)Fx' is a ___ quantification.
44. Groupers show it.
47. Costly
49. 'Some X are Y' converts to 'Some Y ___ ___'.
52. 26a disjunct
54. Kind of cycle
56. The tube
58. Iberian copula

chapter ten

Relational Statements

10.1
Symbolization

All of the predicates discussed in earlier chapters have been *property* predicates. A property predicate denotes a property (characteristic, quality, feature, aspect) that an individual may possess. A property predicate and *one* singular term juxtaposed (in a suitable order) form a statement. For example, S1 results from placing together the singular term 'Telly Savalas' and the property predicate 'is bald'.

(S1)   Telly Savalas is bald.

A *relational* predicate denotes a relation that can hold between *two* (or more) individuals. A relational predicate and two (or more) singular terms juxtaposed (in a suitable order) will form a statement. S2 results from placing together the singular terms 'Coral Gables' and 'Key West' and the relational predicate 'is larger than'.

(S2)   Coral Gables is larger than Key West.

This chapter is concerned with the symbolization of statements containing relational predicates. Chapter Eleven discusses the evaluation of arguments which include relational predicates.

Relational predicates (like property predicates) are abbreviated by capital letters. But whereas a property-predicate letter is always followed by one lower-case letter (name or variable), a relational predicate letter is followed by two (or more) lower-case letters. S2 will be symbolized with F2.

(S2) Coral Gables is LARGER$_R$ than Key West.

(F2) Lck

I usually identify a relational predicate by writing it entirely in capitals and appending a subscript R.

A *dyadic* relational predicate is one which can be transformed into a statement by the addition of *two* singular terms, for example, 'is larger than'. Most of the relational predicates we shall consider are dyadic (two-place), but occasionally we will meet three- and four-place predicates. There is no maximum number of places that a predicate can involve. S3 contains the three-place predicate 'borrows . . . from'.

(S3) Jim BORROWED$_R$ the hacksaw from Carmen.

(F3) Bjhc

English relational statements are sometimes expressed in the "active mood" (as in S4) and sometimes in the "passive" mood (as in S5).

(S4) Carol LOVES$_R$ Stewart.

(S5) Stewart is loved by Carol.

We adopt the convention that relational-predicate letters abbreviate predicates expressed in the active mood. For example, L abbreviates 'loves', not 'is loved by'. So both S4 and S5 are symbolized by F4.

(F4) Lcs

F6 symbolizes neither S4 nor S5; it does represent S6.

(F6) Lsc

(S6) Stewart loves Carol.

The order in which lower-case letters follow a relational-predicate letter is crucial.

Many relational symbolizations involve quantifiers. Examples:

Someone HATES$_R$ Max.   ($\exists$x)Hxm

Max hates everyone.   (x)Hmx

Max hates no one.   (x)~Hmx *or* ~(∃x)Hmx

Someone hates himself.   (∃x)Hxx

(UD: people) Some relational statements are symbolized by multiple quantifications.

(S7) Someone hates somebody.

(F7) (∃x)(∃y)Hxy

(S8) Everyone hates everybody.

(F8) (x)(y)Hxy

Two different variable letters are required in the symbolization of S7 and S8. F9 is not an acceptable symbolization of S7.

(F9) (∃x)(∃x)Hxx

F9 is not even well-formed; it violates this formation principle (stated first in section 8.1):

A formula is a wff only if no variable in it lies within the scope of two (or more) quantifiers containing the same variable.

Three of the four variables in F9 lie within the scope of two quantifiers containing *x*.

Special problems arise when relational symbolizations involve both universal and existential quantifiers.

(S10) There is a person   (∃x)(y)Hxy (F10)
       who hates everybody.

       There is a person
       who is hated by   (∃x)(y)Hyx
       everybody.

       Everybody hates at   (x)(∃y)Hxy
       least one person.

(S11) Each person is hated
       by at least one   (x)(∃y)Hyx (F11)
       person.

No two of these four English sentences are logically equivalent, and (of course) no two of the four wffs are equivalent. Not only is the order of variables following the predicate letter crucial (as was noted above), the order of the quantifiers is equally significant (when one is universal and one existential). If we transpose the quantifiers in any of these four wffs we radically change the content of the wff. For example, by switching the quantifiers in F10 we produce F12.

(F12) (y)(∃x)Hxy

F12 does *not* symbolize S10; rather, it symbolizes S11. (F11 and F12 are logically equivalent.)

Relational statements commonly contain both property predicates and relational predicates. Five examples:

Every THIEF can PICK$_R$ any LOCK.	(x)(y) [(Tx & Ly) → Pxy] *or* (x) [Tx → (y)(Ly → Pxy)]
There is a thief who can pick some lock.	(∃x)(∃y)(Tx & Ly & Pxy) *or* (∃x) [Tx & (∃y)(Ly & Pxy)]
Some thieves can't pick every lock.	(∃x) [Tx & ~(y)(Ly → Pxy)] *or* (∃x)(∃y)(Tx & Ly & ~Pxy)
No thief can pick every lock.	(x) [Tx → ~(y)(Ly → Pxy)] *or* (x) [Tx → (∃y)(Ly & ~Pxy)]
No thief can pick any lock.	(x)(y) [(Tx & Ly) → ~Pxy] *or* (x) [Tx → (y)(Ly → ~Pxy)]

Notice the customary correlation of universal quantifiers with arrows and of existential quantifiers with ampersands.

As in earlier chapters, quantifications with two or more predicates require quantifier-scope groupers. However, when two quantifiers in such a wff have the same scope (except that the first quantifier precedes the scope of the second), *one* pair of quantifier-scope groupers suffices. For example, the following formula is punctuated satisfactorily:

(x)(y)(Rxy → Ryx)

Four more examples occur in the preceding paragraph.

Until you acquire facility at relational symbolization, it's a good idea to pass in several steps from the English sentence to the wff that symbolizes it; for example:

> There is a lock no thief can pick.
>
> There exists an *x* such that *x* is a lock, and no thief can pick *x*.
>
> There exists an *x* such that *x* is a lock, and for any *y*, if *y* is a thief then it's not the case that *y* can pick *x*.
>
> (∃x) [Lx & (y)(Ty → ~Pyx)]

The chart on page 128 symbolizes ten sentences. I recommend studying it until you understand all of the symbolizations.

Ten Relational Symbolizations

SENTENCE	SYMBOLIZATION	DICTIONARY
(Marlin Perkins) "Every animal in the WILD kingdom is an EXPERT$_R$ at something."	(x) [Wx → (∃y)Exy]	UD: animals $Exy = x$ is expert at y
<u>Polio</u> is CAUSED$_R$ by some VIRUS.	(∃x)(Cxp & Vx)	
(Canteen Corp. official) "No MACHINE WORKS$_R$ all the time."	(x) [Mx → ~(y)Wxy]	$Wxy = x$ works at time y
(Poor Richard) "<u>God</u> HELPS$_R$ them that help themselves."	(x)(Hxx → Hgx)	UD: persons
(Children's book) "<u>Benjy</u> LOVED$_R$ everybody in his family and they all loved him."	(x)(Lbx & Lxb)	UD: members of Benjy's family
(Newspaper) "PLAIN-looking girls are more CHEERFUL than BEAUTIFUL ones."	(x)(y) [(Px & By) → Cxy]	UD: girls $Cxy = x$ is more cheerful than y
(Children's book) "No HUMAN being has ever SEEN$_R$ a DINOSAUR."	(x)(y) [(Hx & Dy) → ~Sxy]	
(Ad) "All ANTACIDS are not alike."	(∃x)(∃y)(Ax & Ay & ~Lxy)	$Lxy = x$ is like y
(A.A. principle) "Only a DRUNK can HELP$_R$ another drunk."	(x)(y) [(Dx & Hyx) → Dy]	
(Goldbach's conjecture) "Every EVEN number is the SUM$_R$ of two PRIMES."	(x) [Ex → (∃y)(∃z)(Py & Pz & Sxyz)]	UD: numbers $Sxyz = x$ is the sum of y and z

The location of quantifier-scope groupers is crucial in relational symbolization. Consider this sentence:

He who defiles an Egyptian TOMB, DIES.

($Axy = x$ defiles y) F13 and F15 are correct symbolizations of the sentence, while F14 and F16 are not — this in spite of the fact that F13 and F14 (F15 and F16) differ only in the location of a single bracket!

(F13)	(x)(y) [(Ty & Axy) → Dx]	[correct]
(F14)	(x) [(y)(Ty & Axy) → Dx]	[mistaken]
(F15)	(x) [(∃y)(Ty & Axy) → Dx]	[correct]
(F16)	(x)(∃y) [(Ty & Axy) → Dx]	[mistaken]

Some people are puzzled to learn that F13 and F15 are equivalent wffs and astounded to find out that F14 and F16 are equivalent. F13 and F14 are not equivalent (nor are F15 and F16). Exercises 208 (Chapter Five) and 219 (Chapter Nine) relate to these points.

English relational sentences are often ambiguous; S17 is an example.

(S17)   Some thief can pick any lock.

A person who utters S17 may have in mind S18 or S19.

(S18)   There is a thief who can pick every lock.
(S19)   Any lock can be picked by at least one thief.

S18 entails, but is not entailed by, S19. S18 asserts the existence of an omnicompetent lock picker; S19 does not. The two sentences are readily symbolized.

(F18)   (∃x) [Tx & (y)(Ly → Pxy)]
(F19)   (x) [Lx → (∃y)(Ty & Pyx)]

It is a noteworthy fact about predicate logic that no symbolization of S17 will preserve its ambiguity. In a language of wffs, nothing is ambiguous. Consider another example; S20 was part of a public-service announcement on television.

(S20)   "Someone knows about every child that's neglected."

S20 could be construed as equivalent to S21 or S22; but we all view it as synonymous with S21, perhaps because S22 is so clearly false.

> (S21)   Each case of child neglect is known by at least one person.

> (S22)   There is a person who knows of all cases of child neglect.

10.2
Properties of Relations

Relations have properties. Some of these properties are of particular interest to logicians; they are the subject of this section. We will concentrate on properties of *dyadic* relations.

Some relations have the following characteristic:

> **If any individual bears the relation to a second individual, then the second bears it to the first.**

Logicians call this characteristic "symmetry." An example: If Anna is a cousin of Belle, then Belle must be a cousin of Anna. "Being cousin of" is a symmetrical relation. Other symmetrical relations include "touching" and "being a coauthor with." We now have a symbolic language rich enough to allow the symbolization of statements which attribute symmetry, S1 for example.

> (S1)   "Being $COUSIN_R$ of" is a symmetrical relation.

> (F1) $(x)(y)(Cxy \rightarrow Cyx)$

Some relations are "asymmetrical." A definition of this notion:

> **A relation, R, is asymmetrical iff, if any individual bears R to a second, then the second does not bear R to the first.**

"Weighing more than" is an asymmetrical relation. If Scout weighs more than Tiger, then Tiger cannot weigh more than Scout. Other asymmetrical relations: "being a child of" and "being north of." S2 is symbolized by F2.

> (S2)   "$WEIGHING_R$ more than" is an asymmetrical relation.

> (F2) $(x)(y)(Wxy \rightarrow {\sim}Wyx)$

We will call a relation which is neither symmetrical nor asymmetrical "nonsymmetrical." "Loving," "seeing," and "being brother of" are nonsymmetrical relations. S3 may be symbolized by F3 or (its logical equivalent) F3'.

(S3) "LOVING"$_R$ is a nonsymmetrical relation.

(F3) ~(x)(y)(Lxy → Lyx) & ~(x)(y)(Lxy → ~Lyx)

(F3') (∃x)(∃y)(Lxy & ~Lyx) & (∃x)(∃y)(Lxy & Lyx)

We turn to a second group of properties: "transitivity," "intransitivity," and "nontransitivity." A "transitive" relation exhibits this property:

If any individual bears this relation to a second and the second bears it to a third, then the first bears it to the third.

"Being greater than" is a transitive relation; if five is greater than three and three greater than one, then five must be greater than one. Other transitive relations: "being an ancestor of" and "moving faster than." F4 symbolizes S4.

(S4) "Being GREATER$_R$ than" is a transitive relation.

(F4) (x)(y)(z) [(Gxy & Gyz) → Gxz]

A definition of "intransitivity":

A relation, *R*, is intransitive iff, if any individual bears *R* to a second and the second bears *R* to a third, then the first does not bear *R* to the third.

"Being father of" is intransitive; if Art is the father of Brad and Brad the father of Clark, then Art cannot be Clark's father.[1] "Being two inches taller than" and "being the immediate successor of" are intransitive relations. S5 is symbolized by F5.

(S5) "Being FATHER$_R$ of" is an intransitive relation.

(F5) (x)(y)(z) [(Fxy & Fyz) → ~Fxz]

A relation which is neither transitive nor intransitive is "nontransitive." "Admiring," "being ten feet from," and "fearing" are sample nontransitive relations. S6 may be symbolized by F6 or F6'.

(S6) "ADMIRING"$_R$ is a nontransitive relation.

(F6) ~(x)(y)(z) [(Axy & Ayz) → Axz] & ~(x)(y)(z) [(Axy & Ayz) → ~Axz]

(F6') (∃x)(∃y)(∃z)(Axy & Ayz & ~Axz) & (∃x)(∃y)(∃z)(Axy & Ayz & Axz)

I will explain one more set of properties: "total reflexivity," "reflexivity," "irreflexivity," and "nonreflexivity."

---

[1] The predicate 'is father of' may designate a biological or a legal relationship; the properties of these two relations differ. In the example above I speak of the biological relation.

> **A relation, _R_, is totally reflexive iff every individual bears _R_ to itself.**

"Being identical with" is totally reflexive; every individual is identical with itself. F7 symbolizes S7.

> (S7) "IDENTITY"$_R$ is a totally reflexive relation.
>
> (F7) (x)Ixx

Total reflexivity is rare; "plain" reflexivity is more common.

> **A relation, _R_, is reflexive iff any individual that enters into the relation bears _R_ to itself.**

"Entailment" is a reflexive relation. Not everything entails itself (Boston does not entail itself), so entailment is not _totally_ reflexive,[2] but anything that entails or is entailed by other individuals entails itself. "Being divisible by" is another reflexive relation. S8 is symbolized by F8.

> (S8) "ENTAILMENT"$_R$ is a reflexive relation.
>
> (F8) (x)(y) [(Exy ∨ Eyx) → Exx]

Every totally reflexive relation is reflexive.
    "Irreflexivity" defined:

> **A relation, _R_, is irreflexive iff no individual bears _R_ to itself.**

"Being mother of" is an irreflexive relation; no woman is her own mother. "Standing next to" is also irreflexive. F9 symbolizes S9.

> (S9) "Being MOTHER$_R$ of" is an irreflexive relation.
>
> (F9) (x)~Mxx

A relation which is neither reflexive nor irreflexive is "nonreflexive." "Killing" and "respecting" are nonreflexive relations. Some who kill others do not kill themselves (so "killing" is not reflexive) and some people commit suicide (so "killing" is not irreflexive). S10 is symbolized by F10.

> (S10) "KILLING"$_R$ is a nonreflexive relation.
>
> (F10) (∃x)(∃y) [(Kxy ∨ Kyx) & ~Kxx] & (∃x)Kxx

Every dyadic relation has at least one (and usually _exactly_ one) property from the "symmetry" group, at least one from the "transitivity" set, and at least one from the "reflexivity" group. "Being older than," for

---

[2] My remarks presuppose a UD of everything. For a UD of statements, "entailment" _is_ totally reflexive.

example, is asymmetrical, transitive, and irreflexive. Some of the logical connections which hold between these ten properties will be explored in Chapter Eleven.

EXERCISES

83. Symbolize these statements.

    (a) Some PERSON KNOWS$_R$ some SONG.

    (b) Every person knows at least one song.

    (c) Every person knows every song.

  *(d) There is a person who knows no songs.

    (e) There is a person who does not know all songs.

84. Translate each wff into a colloquial English sentence using the dictionary provided.

    $Tx = x$ is a teacher

    $Sx = x$ is a student

    $Bxy = x$ bores y

    (a) $(\exists x)(\exists y)(Tx \mathrel{\&} Sy \mathrel{\&} Bxy)$

    (b) $(\exists x)(\exists y)(Tx \mathrel{\&} Sy \mathrel{\&} {\sim}Bxy)$

    (c) $(\exists x)[Tx \mathrel{\&} (y)(Sy \rightarrow Bxy)]$

  *(d) $(\exists x)[Tx \mathrel{\&} (y)(Sy \rightarrow Byx)]$

    (e) $(\exists x)[Sx \mathrel{\&} (y)(Ty \rightarrow {\sim}Byx)]$

    (f) $(x)(y)[(Tx \mathrel{\&} Sy) \rightarrow Byx]$

85. A logic-text manuscript I reviewed contained these sample symbolizations:

    (S1)   Some PERSON HAS$_R$ all the CHIPS.
    (F4) $(x)[Cx \rightarrow (\exists y)(Py \mathrel{\&} Hyx)]$

    (S2)   No person has any MONEY.
    (F5) $(x)[Mx \rightarrow (\exists y)(Py \mathrel{\&} {\sim}Hyx)]$

    (S3)   No person has all the chips.
    (F6) $(x)(y)[(Px \mathrel{\&} Cy) \rightarrow {\sim}Hxy]$

All of these symbolizations are mistaken! Symbolize S1 through S3. Translate F4 through F6 into colloquial English sentences.

Instructions for exercises 86, 87, and 221 through 223: Symbolize the statements.

86. (a) "Logical EQUIVALENCE"$_R$ is a symmetrical relation.

    (b) "Logical equivalence" is a transitive relation.

    (c) "Logical equivalence" is a reflexive relation.

(d) "Being two inches TALLER$_R$ than" is an asymmetrical relation.

(e) "Being two inches taller than" is an intransitive relation.

(f) "Being two inches taller than" is an irreflexive relation.

87. For sentences (a) through (h) the UD is people.

   (a) *(Newspaper)* "[In today's society], everybody SUES$_R$ everybody."

   (b) *(Song title)* "Everybody's somebody's FOOL$_R$." *(Fxy = x is y's fool)*

   (c) *(Children's book)* "Georgie never SCARED$_R$ anybody."

   *(d) *(Sign in gas station)* "No one can PLEASE$_R$ everybody."

   (e) *(Newspaper)* "Everybody LOVES$_R$ a man who has GASOLINE for sale."

   (f) *(Boswell)* "One does not LIKE$_R$ those whom one has greatly IN-JURED$_R$."

   (g) *(Samuel Johnson)* "Every man KNOWS$_R$ some whom he cannot induce himself to TRUST$_R$."

   (h) *(Radio newscast)* "Everyone in Huntsville KNEW$_R$ at least some of the HOSTAGES." *(Rx = x is a resident of Huntsville)*

   (i) There is a SCHOOL with only BLACK PUPILS$_R$. *(Pxy = x is a pupil in y)*

   *(j) *(Abby)* "No one can be HAPPY$_R$ with a SLOB but another slob." (UD: people; *Hxy = x lives happily with y)*

   (k) *(Children's book)* "In all FRANCE there was no MOUSE more BE-LOVED$_R$ than Anatole." *(Fx = x resides in France, Bxy = x is more beloved than y)*

   *(l) *(Book)* "Other whales are afraid of KILLER whales." (UD: whales; *Fxy = x fears y)*

   *(m) *(Gypsy woman in* Wolfman*)* "Whoever is BITTEN$_R$ by a WEREWOLF and LIVES becomes a werewolf himself." (UD: people; *Ax = x becomes a werewolf)*

   (n) *(Magazine ad)* "Some CHILDREN WEAR$_R$ nothing but Florence EISEMAN clothes." *(Ex = x is manufactured by Florence Eiseman, Ax = x is an article of clothing)*

   (o) *(Dean Martin's theme)* "Everybody LOVES$_R$ somebody sometime." *(Px = x is a person, Lxyz = x loves y at time z)*

221. (CHALLENGING) For sentences (a) through (h) the UD is people.

   (a) *(Folklore)* "Any seventh SON$_R$ of a seventh son can HEAL." *(Sxy = x is the seventh son of y)*

   (b) *(Aphorism)* "Any LAWYER who represents himself has a FOOL for a CLIENT$_R$." *(Cxy = x is a client of y)*

   (c) Every person who commits suicide commits homicide. (Use one predicate: *Kxy = x kills y.)*

(d) *(Newspaper)* "Marriages are PERMITTED$_R$ only between a MAN and a WOMAN." ($Pxy = x$ is permitted to marry y)

(e) *(Book)* "If any TEACHER finds himself DISLIKING$_R$ all his PUPILS$_R$, he should change his CHARACTER." ($Pxy = x$ is a pupil of y, $Cx = x$ should change his character)

(f) *(Jewish law)* "A JEW is a person who was born of a Jewish MOTHER$_R$, and who never left his faith by ACCEPTING another religion, or one who has accepted the Jewish faith by an official CONVERSION-to-Judaism ceremony." ($Ax = x$ has accepted a religion other than Judaism, $Cx = x$ has converted to Judaism by official ceremony)

(g) "Every MOTHER$_R$ has the right to give ADVICE$_R$ to any mother's child." (Use only two predicates.)

May 7, 1971, Field Enterprises, Inc.

(h) "A MEKEO tribesman of New Guinea wears a TURTLE shell disk on his forehead only if he — or an ANCESTOR$_R$ — has KILLED an enemy in battle." ($Kx = x$ has killed some enemy in battle)

© King Features Syndicate, 1974.

(i) All DETERGENTS CONTAINING$_R$ any PHOSPHORUS are BANNED.

(j) *(ACLU slogan)* "What may be DONE$_R$ to one may be done to all." *(Dxy =x* may be done to *y, Px =x* is a person)

(k) No SYSTEM which has either an all-black or an all-white school is UNITARY. *(Axy =x* is part of *y, Bx =x* is black, *Wx =x* is white, *Pxy =x* is a pupil at *y, Cx =x* is a school)

(l) *(Geoffrey Hunter)* "So far as LOGIC and MATHEMATICS are concerned, whatever can be SAID$_R$ in some existing NATURAL language or other can be said in some one existing natural language." *(Lx =x* pertains to logic, *Mx =x* pertains to mathematics, *Sxy =x* can be said in *y, Nx =x* is a natural language)

222. (CHALLENGING) (a) Symbolize this sentence:

There is a PELICAN ON$_R$ every piling.

(Oxy =x is on *y, Ax =x* is a piling) (b) There is a second (very unusual) meaning this sentence might have. (Imagine a huge pelican and contiguous pilings.) Symbolize the sentence interpreted in this way.

223. (CHALLENGING) The definition of 'adultery' varies from state to state.[3] Here are three such definitions:

(S1) An adulterer is a married person who has intercourse with someone other than his or her spouse.

(S2) An adulterer is either a person who has intercourse with someone married to another or a married person who has intercourse with someone other than his or her spouse.

(S3) An adulterer is either a man who has intercourse with a woman married to another or a married woman who has intercourse with a man other than her husband.

Symbolize these definitions. (UD: people; *Ax =x* is an adulterer, *Mxy =x* is married to *y, Ixy =x* has intercourse with *y, Bx =x* is a man, *Wx =x* is a woman) *B* and *W* are required for the symbolization of S3 only.

224. (CHALLENGING) Sign in a Seven-Eleven convenience store:

Colder beer than ours . . . there ain't.

Two putative symbolizations:

(F1) (x)(y) [(Sx & ~Sy) → Cxy]

(F2) (x)(y) [(Sx & ~Sy) → ~Cyx]

(UD: beer; *Sx =x* is sold at a Seven-Eleven store, *Cxy =x* is colder than *y*) One of these wffs correctly symbolizes the sign, the other does not. (a) Which one is correct? (b) Why is the other incorrect?

[3] See "Appeals Court Defines Adultery" (Associated Press), *Miami News*, March 12, 1975, p. 2-A.

Two of my logic students offered F4 and F5 as symbolizations of S3.

(S3)   There are no smallest particles of MATTER.

(F4) $\sim(\exists x)[Mx \ \& \ (y)(My \rightarrow Sxy)]$

(F5) $\sim(\exists x)[Mx \ \& \ (y)(My \rightarrow \sim Syx)]$

($Sxy = x$ is smaller than y) One of these symbolizations is correct and one is not. (c) Which one is correct? (d) Why is the other incorrect?

225. (CHALLENGING) Cite a relation which is *both* transitive and intransitive. Explain how it can be both.

10.3
Definitions

Throughout the book I have used the concept of a "well-formed formula"; but this important concept has not yet been defined. In section 10.1, I completed our predicate-logic vocabulary by introducing relational predicates. Now it is possible to define 'well-formed formula' for predicate logic. Devising this definition is the main point of the present section; presenting a definition of the notion of "quantifier scope" is another important part of the section. I'm afraid that this section is the driest and most tedious one in the book. As the material presented here is not presupposed by the remainder of the book, some readers will prefer to skip the section.

Before defining 'wff' we need to define the broader notion of 'formula'. Wffs are a species of formula, namely, formulas constructed according to the rules of logical grammar. The following eight definitions culminate in a definition of 'formula'. The symbol '$=_{df}$' is short for 'equals by definition'.

capital	$=_{df}$	an upper-case letter of the English alphabet
variable	$=_{df}$	a lower-case ex, wye, or zee (with or without one or more prime marks)
name	$=_{df}$	a lower-case letter of the English alphabet other than a variable
reverse-E	$=_{df}$	the mark '$\exists$'
connective	$=_{df}$	an arrow, ampersand, double arrow, wedge, or tilde
grouper	$=_{df}$	a parenthesis, bracket, or brace
symbol	$=_{df}$	a capital, variable, name, reverse-E, connective, or grouper
formula	$=_{df}$	a symbol or a horizontal finite string of symbols

Each of the following counts as a formula:

> A
> (x)Fx
> ∃ & x
> & c K

Only the first two of these formulas are well-formed.

To pave the way for the definition of 'wff', seven terms which will appear in that definition must themselves be defined.

simple statement	=_{df}	a capital or a capital followed by one or more names
left-hand grouper	=_{df}	either the mark '(' or '[' or '{'
matching right-hand grouper	=_{df}	the mirror image of a left-hand grouper
dyadic connective	=_{df}	connective other than the tilde
existential quantifier	=_{df}	a left parenthesis followed by a reverse-E followed by a variable followed by a right parenthesis
universal quantifier	=_{df}	a left parenthesis followed by a variable followed by a right parenthesis
quantifier	=_{df}	an existential or universal quantifier

With the aid of these preliminary definitions, it is possible to provide this relatively short recursive definition of 'wff':[4]

> wff =_{df} (i) a simple statement, or
> (ii) a tilde followed by a wff, or
> (iii) a left-hand grouper followed by a wff followed by a dyadic connective followed by another wff followed by a matching right-hand grouper, or
> (iv) a formula which can be generated from a wff by prefixing a quantifier (whose variable, v, does not occur in the wff) and replacing at least one occurrence of a name by v.

By applying this definition we can decide for any given formula whether it is well-formed. I will give several examples, beginning with F1.

> (F1) P

F1 is a simple statement and so, by clause (i) of the definition of 'wff', it is a wff. F1 is a wff of propositional logic; in fact, every wff of proposi-

---

[4]In constructing this definition I have depended heavily on the account given in Lemmon, *Beginning Logic*, pp. 138–142. My definition of 'quantifier scope' is derived from the same source (pp. 143–144).

tional logic will also be a wff of predicate logic. Predicate logic may be viewed as an extension of propositional logic.

(F2)   & Q

F2 is not covered by any of the clauses of the definition; therefore, it is not a wff.

Clause (iv) of the definition covers quantifications. Let's see how it applies to F3.

(F3)   (x)(Ax → Bx)

(F4)   (Ac → Bc)

By clauses (i) and (iii), F4 counts as a wff. F3 can be generated from F4 in the way described by clause (iv); hence, F3 is a wff. F5 is a more complex example.

(F5)   (∃x)~(∃y)Rxy

(F6)   Rab

(F7)   (∃y)Ray

(F8)   ~(∃y)Ray

F6 is a wff according to clause (i). As F7 can be generated from F6 following the directions contained in clause (iv), F7 is also a wff. Then by clause (ii), F8 is a wff. Finally, since F5 can be generated from F8, F5 is a wff by virtue of clause (iv).

The definition of 'wff' has these consequences:

Every quantifier in a wff binds some variable (in addition to the occurrence of the variable within the quantifier).

Every variable in a wff is bound by some quantifier.

No variable in a wff is bound by two quantifiers.

Because of the first of these consequences, F9 is not a wff.

(F9)   (x)Ca

Let's note how the definition of 'wff' excludes F9. None of the first three clauses covers the formula. Nor does the fourth clause apply, for that clause specifies that the variable in the quantifier must also appear later in the formula. F9, then, is not a wff. F10 violates the second consequence.

(F10)   (x)Rxy

If F10 qualifies as a wff, it must do so in virtue of clause (iv). F10 can be generated (in the way described in that clause) only from a formula such as F11.

(F11) Ray

But F11, itself, is not a wff. Therefore, F10 fails to be a wff. F12 violates the third consequence.

(F12) $(\exists x)(x)Cx$

If any clause applies to F12, it is (iv). F12 can only be generated from a formula such as F9. But F9 (as we saw above) is no wff; thus F12 also is not a wff.

With a few minor exceptions pertaining to groupers, the formation principles laid down in the definition of 'wff' correspond to our practices of wff construction throughout the book. That is, the formulas we have recognized as wffs all along satisfy this definition, and the formulas we have viewed as improperly constructed fail to satisfy the definition. It is a remarkable fact that such a concise definition can serve to subdivide satisfactorily the infinitely large class of formulas into the two (infinite) subclasses of wffs and non-wffs.

In section 5.1 I promised to provide (in the present section) a precise definition of the concept of "quantifier scope." This notion is critical because it is presupposed by the statement of the UO, EO, and QE rules of inference. UO and QE speak of "universal quantifications" and EO and QE speak of "existential quantifications." These concepts were defined (in section 5.1) as follows:

> A universal quantification is a wff beginning with a universal quantifier whose scope is the entire wff.

> An existential quantification is a wff beginning with an existential quantifier whose scope is the entire wff.

The notion of "quantifier scope" has been explained roughly, but until now it has not been formally defined. The precision of the rules UO, EO, and QE requires that 'quantifier scope' be exactly defined.

Before producing a definition of 'quantifier scope', we must define 'propositional function':

> **A propositional function is a formula which results when zero or more (contiguous) quantifiers are deleted from the front of a formula which is a wff under clause (iv) of the definition of 'wff'.**

Some propositional functions are wffs, others are not. Examples:

(x)(∃y)Rxy   [wff]
(∃y)Rxy   [non-wff]
Rxy   [non-wff]

The definition of 'quantifier scope':

The scope of a quantifier in a wff is the shortest propositional function in which it occurs (provided that the next symbol, if any, in the wff is neither a variable nor a name).[5]

I apply this definition to F13.

(F13)   (∃x)[(y)Rxy → Fx]

The shortest propositional function in which the universal quantifier occurs is F14. Accordingly, F14 is the scope of that quantifier.

(F14)   (y)Rxy

We know that F14 is a propositional function because it results from deleting the initial quantifier of (for instance) F15, which is a wff by clause (iv) of the definition of 'wff'.

(F15)   (x)(y)Rxy

The shortest propositional function in which the existential quantifier of F13 occurs is F13, itself. F13, then, is the scope of that quantifier. The scope of the existential quantifier in F13 cannot be, for example, F16 because F16 is not a propositional function.

(F16)   (∃x)[(y)Rxy

---

[5]The parenthetical clause is included so that (for example) the scope of the second quantifier in '(x)(y)Ryx' will be '(y)Ryx' and not just '(y)Ry'.

chapter eleven

Relational
Arguments

11.1
Proofs

In this chapter we discuss the evaluation of arguments involving relations. Section 11.1 treats formal proofs for such arguments and 11.2 concerns the method of interpretation as applied to relational arguments.

The formal-proof procedure already developed is adequate to the
task of validating relational arguments. I will illustrate this by constructing proofs for several arguments. The first argument occurs in the movie
"Dracula's Daughter" (1936). The old professor has killed Count Dracula
by driving a wooden stake through his heart. His younger colleague (un-
aware that the count was a vampire) offers to speak on the old man's
behalf at the trial.

> YOUNG PROFESSOR: *"I'll tell the court you're insane."*
>
> OLD PROFESSOR: *"But I'm not insane."*
>
> YOUNG PROFESSOR: *"Then you are guilty of murder!"*
>
> OLD PROFESSOR: *"You can't murder a man who has been dead for 500 years."*

The older man's argument:

> No one can MURDER$_R$ a person who has been dead FIVE hundred years. Count <u>Dracula</u> has been dead that long. Therefore, I have not murdered him.

In symbols:

$$(x)[Fx \rightarrow (y){\sim}Myx], \ Fd \vdash {\sim}Mpd$$

(UD: people; $p =$ the old professor) A formal proof:

(1)	$(x)[Fx \rightarrow (y){\sim}Myx]$	A
(2)	Fd	A
(3)	$Fd \rightarrow (y){\sim}Myd$	1 UO
(4)	$(y){\sim}Myd$	3,2 $\rightarrow$O
(5)	${\sim}Mpd$	4 UO

In deriving line 3 the UO Rule is applied to line 1 — a quantification containing *two* quantifiers. This requires a slight modification in the definition of *instance*. I italicize the added words.

> **An instance of a universal quantification is a wff which results from (a) deleting the *initial* quantifier and (b) replacing each of the remaining occurrences of the *initial-quantifier* variable by the same name.**

An instance of an existential quantification is explained analogously. Returning to the proof — line 3 is reached by eliminating the first quantifier on line 1 and replacing the two remaining x's by d's. The two y's remain untouched. I selected d for the instance on line 3 so that the antecedent of that line will match line 2. Note that the UO Rule does not apply to line 3 (because 3 is not a universal quantification).

A second example:

> Nothing CREATED$_R$ <u>God</u>. So, He did not create everything.

Symbolized:

$${\sim}(\exists x)Cxg \vdash {\sim}(x)Cgx$$

As the conclusion of the argument is the negation of a quantification, the basic pattern of the proof will be Tilde In. The proof begins:

(1)	${\sim}(\exists x)Cxg$	A
(2)	$(x)Cgx$	PA
(3)	$(x){\sim}Cxg$	1 QE

Lines 4 and 5 obviously will be derived from lines 2 and 3 by means of the UO Rule. Since UO (unlike EO) is an unrestricted rule, I can instantiate to any name or pair of names on lines 4 and 5. Suppose I instantiate to *a* on both lines:

(4) Cga   2 UO
(5) ~Cag   3 UO

I have made no logical error here, but I have made a *strategic* mistake. Because this is a Tilde In proof, I must reach a standard contradiction. However, 'Cga & ~Cag' is not a standard contradiction. It isn't a contradiction at all; there's nothing contradictory about the statement: 'g created *a* but *a* did not create g'. After studying the matter I conclude that in order to reach a standard contradiction I must instantiate to g on both lines 4 and 5. The proof in its entirety:

(1) ~(∃x)Cxg   A
(2) (x)Cgx   PA
(3) (x)~Cxg   1 QE
(4) Cgg   2 UO
(5) ~Cgg   3 UO
(6) Cgg & ~Cgg   4,5 &I
(7) ~(x)Cgx   2–6 ~I

Note that line 6 *is* a standard contradiction.

A third example is suggested by this statement by the lexicographer H. W. Fowler:

> *Synonyms, in the narrowest sense, are separate words whose meaning . . . is so fully identical that one can always be substituted for the other without change in the effect of the sentence in which it is done. Whether any such perfect synonyms exist is doubtful. . . .*[1]

An argument based on this passage:

> One word is a PERFECT synonym of another iff the first can be SUBSTITUTED for the second in any sentence without changing the effect of that sentence. Since there is no pair of words which can be so interchanged, it follows that there are no perfectly synonymous words.

Symbolized:

(x)(y)(Pxy ↔ Sxy), ~(∃x)(∃y)Sxy ⊢ ~(∃x)(∃y)Pxy

---

[1] H. W. Fowler, *A Dictionary of Modern English Usage* (Oxford: Oxford University Press, 1950), p. 591.

(UD: words; $Sxy = x$ can be substituted for y in any sentence without changing the effect of the sentence) A formal proof of this argument:

(1)	$(x)(y)(Pxy \leftrightarrow Sxy)$	A
(2)	$\sim(\exists x)(\exists y)Sxy$	A
(3)	$(\exists x)(\exists y)Pxy$	PA
(4)	$(\exists y)Pay$	3 EO
(5)	Pab	4 EO
(6)	$(y)(Pay \leftrightarrow Say)$	1 UO
(7)	$Pab \leftrightarrow Sab$	6 UO
(8)	$(x)\sim(\exists y)Sxy$	2 QE
(9)	$\sim(\exists y)Say$	8 UO
(10)	$(y)\sim Say$	9 QE
(11)	$\sim Sab$	10 UO
(12)	$Pab \rightarrow Sab$	7 $\leftrightarrow$O
(13)	Sab	12,5 $\rightarrow$O
(14)	Sab & $\sim Sab$	13,11 &I
(15)	$\sim(\exists x)(\exists y)Pxy$	3–14 $\sim$I

Some comments about this proof: One of the restrictions on the EO Rule is that the name introduced may not appear on any line above the line derived. Hence the third letter in the wff on line 5 must be a name other than a (since a occurs on line 4). Line 6 is derived from line 1 by the UO Rule. There are no restrictions on UO, so I was free to instantiate to *any* name on line 6. However, by casting an eye on line 5 (where the predicate P is followed by the name a), I determined that instantiating to a on line 6 would help complete the proof. Similar reasoning determined the selection of names for the instantiations on lines 7, 9, and 11.

Proofs of relational arguments are often lengthy. In order to avoid unnecessary length, I suggest the adoption of three shortcuts—one related to each of these rules of inference: UO, EO, and QE. These shortcuts will be illustrated by reference to the proof just presented.

The first shortcut is the *multiple application of UO*. When a universal quantification begins with two or more contiguous universal quantifiers, all of those quantifiers may be dropped in one step of UO. For example, we may apply this shortcut to the first line of the above proof.

(1)	$(x)(y)(Pxy \leftrightarrow Sxy)$	A
	•	
	•	
	•	
(6)	$Pab \leftrightarrow Sab$	1 UO

If pressed to justify this shortcut in a given proof, we could do so by showing how to reach the same instantiation through several steps of UO. Universal quantifiers cannot be eliminated in this way if they are preceded by *any* symbol other than universal quantifiers. So the shortcut cannot be correctly applied to any of the following wffs:

> ~(x)(y)Rxy
> (x)~(y)Rxy
> (x)[(y)Rxy → Fx]
> (x)(∃y)(z)Rxyz

Obviously the shortcut applies only to universal quantifications; it could not be used with this wff (which is a conditional — not a universal quantification):

> (x)(y)Rxy → Fa

The second shortcut I propose is the *multiple application of EO.* When an existential quantification begins with two or more contiguous existential quantifiers, all of those quantifiers may be eliminated in one step of EO. The shortcut may be applied to line 3 of the proof.

> (3) (∃x)(∃y)Pxy   PA
> •
> •
> •
> (5) Pab   3 EO

Existential quantifiers cannot be eliminated in this manner if they are preceded by any symbol other than existential quantifiers. The familiar restrictions on the EO Rule must be observed: the names introduced may not occur (1) in the symbolization of the argument or (2) on any line above the line derived. In addition, we must observe one more restriction when we use the EO shortcut: different variables (x and y, for example) must be replaced by different names. Thus it would be mistaken to pass from line 3 to:

> (5) Paa   3 EO (ERROR!)

The last shortcut involves *quantifier exchange.* To license this maneuver we need to reformulate the QE Rule:

> **The Relaxed Quantifier Exchange Rule (QE): From a wff which begins with a tilde followed by two or more contiguous quantifiers (call them C-quantifiers) whose scope includes the remainder of the wff, derive the wff which results from (1) deleting the tilde, (2) replacing each**

universal *C*-quantifier by an existential quantifier (involving the same variable), (3) replacing each existential *C*-quantifier by a universal quantifier (involving the same variable), and (4) inserting a tilde after the last replaced *C*-quantifier.

The statement of this rule is complex but the idea is simple, as these examples will show:

> (2) $\sim(\exists x)(\exists y)Sxy$ A
>
> •
>
> •
>
> •
>
> (4) $(x)(y)\sim Sxy$ 2 QE

> (12) $\sim(x)(\exists y)(z)Rxyz$
>
> (13) $(\exists x)(y)(\exists z)\sim Rxyz$ 12 QE

The Relaxed QE Rule is a derived rule of inference in this sense: any wff which can be deduced with its aid could be reached in a more roundabout fashion with our other rules of inference (including the more stringent version of QE). The Relaxed QE Rule may not be applied to wffs where the quantifiers involved are separated by symbols other than quantifiers. For example, it cannot be applied correctly to these formulas:

> $\sim(x)\sim(\exists y)Rxy$
>
> $\sim(x)[(y)Rxy \rightarrow Fx]$

When all three shortcuts are employed in a proof of the "synonym" argument, four lines are eliminated. (In some proofs greater economies will result.)

> (1) $(x)(y)(Pxy \leftrightarrow Sxy)$ A
>
> (2) $\sim(\exists x)(\exists y)Sxy$ A
>
> (3) $(\exists x)(\exists y)Pxy$ PA
>
> (4) $(x)(y)\sim Sxy$ 2 QE
>
> (5) Pab   3 EO
>
> (6) Pab $\leftrightarrow$ Sab   1 UO
>
> (7) $\sim$Sab   4 UO
>
> (8) Pab $\rightarrow$ Sab   6 $\leftrightarrow$O
>
> (9) Sab   8,5 $\rightarrow$O
>
> (10) Sab & $\sim$Sab   9,7 &I
>
> (11) $\sim(\exists x)(\exists y)Pxy$ 3–10 $\sim$I

At the conclusion of section 10.2 I remarked that the properties of relations discussed there are logically connected to each other. This argument concerns the connection between asymmetry and irreflexivity:

"WEIGHING$_R$ more than" is an asymmetrical relation. Thus, it is an irreflexive relation.

Symbolized:

$(x)(y)(Wxy \rightarrow \sim Wyx) \vdash (x)\sim Wxx$

A formal proof:

(1) $(x)(y)(Wxy \rightarrow \sim Wyx)$ A
(2) $\sim(x)\sim Wxx$ PA
(3) $(\exists x)\sim\sim Wxx$ 2 QE
(4) $\sim\sim Waa$ 3 EO
(5) $Waa \rightarrow \sim Waa$ 1 UO
(6) $\sim Waa$ 5,4 MT
(7) $\sim Waa$ & $\sim\sim Waa$ 6,4 &I
(8) $(x)\sim Wxx$ 2-7 $\sim$O

This argument treats the relation of "weighing more than," but it is clear that a similar proof can be constructed for any asymmetrical relation. Thus we have shown more generally that all asymmetrical relations are irreflexive. Line 5 is derived by taking a UO shortcut. Notice that I instantiated both the x and y variables in line 1 to the name a on line 5. This is permitted (but it would be prohibited had the step involved an EO shortcut). If I had instantiated to anything other than two a's on line 5, I could not have derived line 6 from lines 5 and 4.

In section 2.3 I promised to validate this argument:

Each of the first three statements in the list is logically EQUIVALENT$_R$ to the statement directly beneath it. Therefore, the fourth statement is logically equivalent to the first.

That promise will now be fulfilled. But first, two suppressed premises of the argument must be supplied:

"Logical equivalence" is a transitive relation. It is also a symmetrical relation.

(Relational arguments often involve unstated premises like these — that is, premises which ascribe to relations the properties discussed in section 10.2.) If we name the four listed statements a, b, c, and d, we may symbolize the argument in this way:

Eab & Ebc & Ecd, (x)(y)(z)[(Exy & Eyz) → Exz], (x)(y)(Exy → Eyx) ⊢Eda

(UD: statements) A proof:

(1)	Eab & Ebc & Ecd	A
(2)	(x)(y)(z)[(Exy & Eyz) → Exz]	A
(3)	(x)(y)(Exy → Eyx)	A
(4)	(Eab & Ebc) → Eac	2 UO
(5)	Eab & Ebc	1 &O
(6)	Eac	4,5 →O
(7)	(Eac & Ecd) → Ead	2 UO
(8)	Ecd	1 &O
(9)	Eac & Ecd	6,8 &I
(10)	Ead	7,9 →O
(11)	Ead → Eda	3 UO
(12)	Eda	11,10 →O

The strategy behind the proof divides into three stages. First I realized that, since E is transitive (premise 2), I could pass from 'Eab & Ebc' to 'Eac'. This part of the strategy is carried out on lines 4 through 6. Next I reasoned that, given the transitivity of E, I could move from 'Eac' and 'Ecd' to 'Ead'. This was done in lines 7 through 10. Finally I saw that because E is symmetrical (premise 3) I could deduce the conclusion, 'Eda', from 'Ead'. This last phase of the proof occupies lines 11 and 12. An unusual feature of this proof is that line 2 is instantiated *twice* (on lines 4 and 7); this is permissible.

Perhaps the most challenging element in devising relational proofs is selecting the appropriate names when instantiating. As with other aspects of proof building, your skills in this area will improve with practice.

11.2
Interpretations

The method of interpretation may be applied to invalid relational arguments; I shall illustrate the technique on several arguments. The first:

Everybody HATES$_R$ Howard Cosell. So, he hates everyone.

Symbolized:

(x)Hxc ⊢ (x)Hcx

(UD: people) We can prove the invalidity of the argument with this interpretation:

UD: positive integers

$Hxy = x$ is equal to or larger than y
$c =$ one

Each positive integer is equal to or larger than one. (T)

Therefore, one is equal to or larger than every positive integer. (F)

As was explained in Chapter Nine, names must be interpreted with singular terms (not predicates) and predicate letters must be interpreted with predicates (not singular terms). Now a further restriction must be introduced: *Property* predicate letters (predicate letters followed by a single lower-case letter) must be interpreted with *property* predicates, and *relational* predicate letters (predicate letters followed by more than one lower-case letter) must be interpreted with *relational* predicates. For example, each of these attempted interpretations violates the restriction and is therefore unacceptable:

$Ax = x$ is mother of y
$Bxy = x$ is female
$Cxy = x$ is greater than 2

(Note that 'is greater than 2' is a *property* predicate.) The restriction on permissible interpretations must be tightened a bit further: A dyadic predicate letter (one followed by two lower-case letters) can be interpreted only by a dyadic relational predicate; a triadic predicate letter requires a triadic relational interpretation—and so on. Hence, neither of these attempted interpretations is correct:

$Dxy = x$ is between y and z
$Exyz = x$ is north of y

In a 1973 news conference, Richard Nixon severely criticized television-network newsmen. When a reporter asked why he was so angry, Nixon replied,

> *Don't get the impression that you arouse my anger. You see, one can only be angry with those he respects.*[2]

Nixon could be construed as arguing:[3]

---

[2] James Reston, "President Holds up Well, but Bristles at Networks" (New York Times News Service), *Miami News*, October 27, 1973, p. 10-A.

[3] A more plausible analysis of Nixon's comment is the (valid) argument which results from switching the second premise and conclusion of the argument displayed above.

One can only be ANGRY$_R$ with those he RESPECTS$_R$. Network NEWS-MEN do not arouse my anger. Hence, I do not respect network newsmen.

Is this argument valid? It is symbolized:

(x)(y)(Axy → Rxy), (x)(Nx → ~Anx) ⊢ (x)(Nx → ~Rnx)

(n = Nixon) This interpretation demonstrates invalidity:

UD: people

$Axy = x$ is mother of y
$Rxy = x$ is a parent of y
$Nx = x$ is female
n = Richard Nixon

A mother of any person is a parent of that person. (T)

Nixon is mother of no females. (T)

Therefore, Nixon is a parent of no females. (F)

Probably the most common form of relational fallacy involves arguments of the following sort:

Every EVENT is CAUSED$_R$ by some event. Consequently, there is an event which causes all events.

Many arguments in philosophy as well as other areas of inquiry exhibit this form or a variation of it.[4] A symbolization of the "event" argument:

(x) [Ex → (∃y)(Ey & Cyx)] ⊢ (∃x) [Ex & (y)(Ey → Cxy)]

The argument's invalidity is established by this interpretation:

UD: integers

$Ex = x$ is an integer
$Cxy = x$ succeeds y

Every integer has some successor. (T)

Therefore, there is an integer which succeeds all integers. (F)

The conclusion of this latter argument is doubly false: it denies the infinity of the set of integers, and it implies that at least one integer succeeds itself!

The basic structure of the "event" argument is made clearer by a symbolization which uses events as UD:

---

[4] Peter Geach discusses this fallacy and cites instances of it in the works of Aristotle, Plato, Berkeley, and Spinoza in *Logic Matters* (Berkeley and Los Angeles: University of California Press, 1972), pp. 1–13.

$$(x)(\exists y)Cyx \vdash (\exists y)(x)Cyx$$

(To make the structure even clearer I use y as the first variable of quantification in symbolizing the conclusion.) The sole difference between the two wffs of this symbolization is the order of the quantifiers. This explains why some logicians call this mistaken argument pattern the "quantifier-shift fallacy." Attempt a formal proof for this argument and see how one of the restrictions on the EO Rule prevents completion of the proof.

The only quantifier shift which is fallacious is a transposition of existential and universal quantifiers in which an existential quantifier moves to the left of a universal quantifier. When the transposition occurs in the other direction, the resulting wff *is* entailed by the original wff. That is, this symbolized argument is valid:

$$(\exists y)(x)Cyx \vdash (x)(\exists y)Cyx$$

Of course, the corresponding English argument is also valid.

There is an event which causes all events. So, every event is caused by some event.

Exercise 91 at the end of the chapter treats this argument. While the premise entails the conclusion, it is clear that the two statements are not equivalent.

The order of (contiguous) quantifiers is not critical when all the quantifiers are universal. For example, these two wffs are logically equivalent:

$$(x)(y)Rxy$$
$$(y)(x)Rxy$$

Also, quantifier order is not critical when all the quantifiers are existential. The following are logically equivalent formulas:

$$(\exists x)(\exists y)Rxy$$
$$(\exists y)(\exists x)Rxy$$

The transposition of contiguous quantifiers changes the content of a wff only when both universal and existential quantifiers are involved.

My final example is more complex than the others. W. T. Jones offers this summary of an argument in Plato's dialogue *Gorgias:*

> *GOOD and BAD are OPPOSITES$_R$; opposites cannot EXIST$_R$ together at the same time in the same object; pleasure and pain do, however, exist in the same object at the same time. Pleasure therefore cannot be [defined as] good nor pain [as] evil.*[5]

[5] *The Classical Mind: A History of Western Philosophy* (2nd ed.; New York: Harcourt Brace Jovanovich, Inc., 1969), p. 160.

For clarity I symbolize this as a three-premise (rather than one-premise) argument:

> (x)(y)[(Gx & By) → Oxy], (x)(y)(z)(Oxy → ~Exyz),
> (∃x)(∃y)(∃z)(Cx & Dy & Exyz) ⊢ ~(x)(Cx ↔ Gx) & ~(x)(Dx ↔ Bx)

(*Exyz* = *x* and *y* exist in *z* at the same time, *Cx* = *x* is pleasant, *Dx* = *x* is painful) An interpretation which establishes invalidity:

> UD: positive integers
>
> > *Gx* = *x* is less than four
> > *Bx* = *x* is greater than four
> > *Oxy* = *x* is less than *y*
> > *Exyz* = *x* equals the sum of *y* and *z*
> > *Cx* = *x* is less than four
> > *Dx* = *x* is less than four
>
> A positive integer less than four is less than any positive integer greater than four. (T)
>
> If one positive integer is less than a second, it's false that the first equals the sum of the second and some third positive integer. (T)
>
> There are two positive integers less than four such that the first equals the sum of the second and some third positive integer. (For example, three equals two plus one.) (T)
>
> Therefore, it is false that a positive integer is less than four iff it is less than four, and it is false that a positive integer is less than four iff it is greater than four. (F)

The conclusion is false because its left conjunct is false (a positive integer *is* less than four iff it is less than four).

In general, the method of interpretation requires more ingenuity when applied to relational arguments than when used with property arguments. To some extent it will be necessary to operate on a trial-and-error basis. When one attempt at finding a suitable interpretation fails, you will need to modify it, or scrap it and begin again.

EXERCISES

88. Complete the following proofs. Every assumption has been identified.

 *(a)   (1)   Rab   A

     (2)   PA

     (3)   2 QE

     (4)   3 UO

       (5)   1,4 &I

       (6) $(\exists x)(\exists y)Rxy$ 2–5 ~O

 (b) (1) $(\exists x)(y)\sim Syx$ A

       (2) $\sim(x)\sim(y)Sxy$ PA

       (3) $(\exists x)\sim\sim(y)Sxy$

       (4) $(y)\sim Sya$

       (5) $\sim\sim(y)Sby$

       (6) $(y)Sby$

       (7) $\sim Sba$

       (8) Sba

       (9) $Sba\ \&\ \sim Sba$

    (10) $(x)\sim(y)Sxy$

Instructions for exercises 89 through 103: Symbolize the arguments and construct proofs for them. All are valid.

89. In August, 1974, Congressman Rhodes was asked by reporters whether Congress could grant immunity from prosecution to Richard Nixon for his involvement in the Watergate affair. Rhodes replied that Congress does not have the authority to grant immunity to anyone for anything. Clearly he was advancing this argument:

    Congress cannot grant <u>Nixon</u> IMMUNITY$_R$ for <u>Watergate</u>, simply because it can't grant immunity to anyone for anything.

    (n = Nixon, Ixy = Congress can grant x immunity for y, w = Watergate)

*90. Will Rogers said:

    I'm not a MEMBER$_R$ of any ORGANIZED party—I'm a Democrat.

    Show that this entails:

    The <u>Democratic</u> Party is not an organized party.

    'Rogers is a Democrat' amounts to 'Rogers is a member of the Democratic Party'. (r = Will Rogers, d = the Democratic Party)

91.   There is an event which CAUSES$_R$ all events. So, every event is caused by some event.

    (UD: events)

92. A poem by R. D. Laing begins:

    I don't RESPECT$_R$ myself
    I can't respect anyone who respects me.[6]

    Prove that the second line entails the first. (UD: people; i = the speaker)

---

[6] R. D. Laing, *Knots* (New York: Random House, 1970), p. 18.

*93. Philosophers W. V. Quine and J. S. Ullian consider this simplistic analysis of "explanation": A sentence explains whatever it implies. They reject the proposal for the following reason:

> *This would count every sentence as its own explanation, since, trivially, every sentence implies itself.[7]*

Their argument:

> Every sentence IMPLIES_R itself. It is false that every sentence is its own explanation. Hence, it is false that a sentence EXPLAINS_R whatever it implies.

(UD: sentences)

94. A banner displayed at a Chiefs-Bears game featured on ABC's "Monday Night Football" bore this message:

> *Will Rogers never met Howard Cosell.*

Those who designed the banner were inviting the audience to reconstruct their inference:

> Will <u>Rogers</u> never MET_R a man he didn't LIKE_R. If Rogers had met <u>Cosell</u>, he wouldn't have liked him. It follows that Will Rogers never met Howard Cosell.

(UD: men)

95. Glanville Williams writing on attempted suicide:

> *The English courts punish this act on the reasoning that every AT-TEMPT_R to commit a CRIME is PUNISHABLE; <u>suicide</u> is a crime; therefore, attempted suicide is punishable.[8]*

($Axy = x$ is an attempt to do y)

*96. Andy Capp reasons:

> [Galatians 6:7] "Whatever a man SOWS_R, that he will also REAP_R." So, if I sow some BOOZE, I'll reap some booze.

($a = $ Andy)

May 11, 1971. © 1971, Daily Mirror Newspapers Ltd. ANDY CAPP by Reggie Smythe. Courtesy of Field Newspaper Syndicate.

[7] *The Web of Belief* (New York: Random House, 1970), p. 76.

[8] *The Sanctity of Life and the Criminal Law* (New York: Alfred A. Knopf, 1970), p. 273.

97. Logicians Karel Lambert and Bas C. van Fraassen claim that "sibling of" is a transitive relation.[9] This argument proves them mistaken:

> Howard is a SIBLING$_R$ of Miriam and Miriam is a sibling of Howard. Nobody is his own sibling. Thus, it is false that "sibling of" is a transitive relation.

(UD: people)

98. When "P.R." discovered that the girl he loves is a prostitute, he wrote Joyce Brothers for advice. Dr. Brothers replied (in part):

> *A person can only give real love to another human being if he or she loves and respects himself or herself. The prostitute hates herself and seeks a life that is self-punishing.*[10]

Her argument:

> One person can LOVE$_R$ another only if he or she loves himself or herself. No PROSTITUTE loves herself. Hence, no prostitute loves anyone.

(UD: people)

99. In this "Steve Canyon" strip Poteet argues:

> Someone has WRITTEN$_R$ about some EXECUTION. So, it's false that you can't write on a subject unless you've experienced it, because no PERSON who has experienced an execution has written about it.

$(Axy = x$ has experienced $y)$

July 10, 1972. © King Features Syndicate 1972.

100. A story in the University of Miami student newspaper about dormitory searches includes these paragraphs:

---

[9] *Derivation and Counterexample: An Introduction to Philosophical Logic* (Encino, California: Dickenson Publishing Company, Inc., 1972), p. 107.

[10] Joyce Brothers, "Call Girl Presents Problems," © King Features Syndicate 1974. *Miami News*, May 21, 1974, p. 7-B.

All the Search and Seizures have been illegal, according to SBG Vice President Sami Burstyn. To be able to search a student's room, an application for authorization to search must be filled out and signed by a magistrate.

None of the "Searches" which have taken place this semester have had a magistrate's signature, simply because the magistrates have not been selected.[11]

Burstyn's argument:

A SEARCH is LEGITIMATE only if some MAGISTRATE APPROVES$_R$ it. Since there are no magistrates, none of the searches are legitimate.

101. This explanation in a children's book is formulated as an argument:

All SOUNDS are CAUSED$_R$ by something MOVING back and forth very fast. When something moves back and forth very fast we say it VIBRATES. So sounds are caused by vibration.[12]

The second premise is a definition.

*102. Steve Allen writes:

Once, hearing a teen-ager say that he did not like jazz music but did like rock-and-roll, I explained to him that rock is merely a subdivision of jazz, that it grew out of jazz.[13]

A formalization of this argument:

All ROCK and roll is JAZZ. It follows that any PERSON who LIKES$_R$ (some) rock and roll likes (some) jazz.

103. Alan Stang writes the following in *American Opinion:*

. . . Any government which hands out so much—"free"—first has to collect it. A government which hands out everything, first has to take everything. And any government big enough to do that is total government—is totalitarian—has total power over you. . . .[14]

A formalization of this argument:

Whatever a GOVERNMENT HANDS$_R$ out it must have TAKEN$_R$. A government which takes everything is totalitarian. Therefore, a government which hands out everything is totalitarian.

($Hxy = x$ hands out y, $Txy = x$ takes y, $Ax = x$ is totalitarian)

Instructions for exercises 104 through 111: Establish the invalidity of each argument by the method of interpretation. (1) Symbolize the argument; (2) specify

[11] Scott Bressler, "'Room Checks' Cover up Illegal Searches," *Miami Hurricane,* September 21, 1971, p. 1.

[12] Illa Podendorf, *The True Book of Sounds We Hear* (Chicago: Children's Press, 1955), p. 8.

[13] Introduction to Thomas Ellis Katen, *Doing Philosophy* (Englewood Cliffs, N.J.: Prentice-Hall, Inc., 1973), p. xix.

[14] "For Workers: A Letter from the Conservative Right," *American Opinion,* September, 1970, p. 75.

a UD; (3) interpret the descriptive symbols; and (4) formulate the reinterpreted argument in English, noting truth values.

104. Every event is CAUSED$_R$ by some event. Hence, every event causes some event.

    (UD: events)

105. One introduction-to-philosophy textbook advances this argument (not stated quite so explicitly, of course):

    Human ACTS are not CAUSED$_R$ by MOTIVES. Thus, human acts are not caused by anything.

106. The "B.C." strip may be viewed as involving this argument:

    Snowflake <u>A</u> is not LIKE$_R$ snowflake <u>B</u>. This shows that no two snowflakes are alike.

    (UD: snowflakes; a = snowflake A, b = snowflake B)

November 27, 1973. By permission of John Hart and Field Enterprises, Inc.

*107. The first draft of a master's thesis I read contained this passage:

    Temporal priority is not essential to the idea of causation. For surely there are events which are temporally prior to other events without being considered as the cause of those events.

    The conclusion of this argument (the first sentence) may be restated 'It is false that every event which CAUSES$_R$ another event is PRIOR$_R$ to that other event'. (UD: events)

108. Flip Wilson once gave Joe Namath this introduction:

    You've heard the old saying about there being a boy for every girl in the world? Well, here's the boy they meant.

    Flip capitalizes on the ambiguity of 'There's a boy for every girl in the world'. The two meanings of this sentence are given in the following argument:

    Each GIRL LOVES$_R$ some BOY. So, there is a boy all girls love.

109. Philosopher Norman Malcolm writes:

> *Bodily sensations are located where they are* felt *to be. People do not feel sensations in their brains. (Brain tissue is actually insensitive.) Therefore, bodily sensations are not brain processes.*[15]

On one interpretation of this passage, Malcolm is arguing:

If a SENSATION is FELT$_R$ to be at a given place, then it is LOCATED$_R$ at that place. No sensation is felt to be in a BRAIN. It follows that sensations are not located in brains.

($Fxy = x$ is felt to be in place y, $Lxy = x$ is located in place y) When the first premise is altered to 'If a sensation is located at a given place, then it is felt to be at that place', the argument becomes valid. Perhaps Malcolm intends this altered premise.

110. St. Thomas Aquinas' third cosmological argument for the existence of God appears to include this inference:[16]

For each CONTINGENT thing there is a time when it does not EXIST$_R$. Hence, there is a time when no contingent thing exists.

($Exy = x$ exists at time y)

*111. During an NBC telecast of a Dodgers vs. Reds game, sportscasters Kurt Gowdy, Tony Kubeck, and Mel Allen made these comments (paraphrased):

(1) Weren't Ken and George teammates somewhere?

(2) I think one of them was at Houston.

(3) Then I guess they were both at Houston.

One of the sportscasters seems to have reasoned as follows:

Ken and George were ON$_R$ some team at the same time. One of them was once on the Houston team. Thus, they were at Houston at the same time.

($Oxyz = $ player x is on team y at time z)

Instructions for exercises 226 through 229: Symbolize the arguments and construct proofs for them. All are valid.

226. (CHALLENGING)

One statement is LOGICALLY$_R$ equivalent to a second iff each EN-TAILS$_R$ the other. Every statement entails any logical TRUTH. Therefore, a logical truth is logically equivalent to any logical truth.

(UD: statements)

---

[15] *Problems of Mind* (New York: Harper & Row, Publishers, 1971), pp. 69–70.

[16] See the *Summa Theologica*, Question 2, Article 3. Aquinas writes: "But it is impossible for these [contingent things] always to exist, for that which can not-be at some time is not. Therefore, if everything can not-be, then at one time there was nothing in existence."

227. (CHALLENGING) "Desiderata" is a document (dated 1692) discovered in Old Saint Paul's Church, Baltimore. It includes this passage:

> *If you compare yourself with others, you may become vain & bitter; for always there will be greater & lesser persons than yourself.*

An argument is suggested:

> If one COMPARES$_R$ himself with GREATER$_R$ people, he will become BITTER. And if one compares himself with lesser people, he will become VAIN. If a person compares himself with others, he will compare himself with some who are greater as well as some who are lesser. Consequently, if you compare yourself with others, you will become vain and bitter.

(UD: people)

228. (CHALLENGING) The sign in the photograph adorns an unfriendly Miami motel. Show that the sign entails each of the following:

(a) No unaccompanied REGISTERED guest is permitted on the PREMISES.

(b) A registered guest none of whose companions is a registered guest is not permitted on the premises.

Depending on how you symbolize this problem it may be necessary to add this auxiliary premise: '"Accompanying" is a symmetrical relation'. (UD: people; $Axy = x$ accompanies y)

229. (CHALLENGING) The following arguments exhibit some of the logical connections which hold between the properties of dyadic relations discussed in section 10.2.

(a) "Being (natural) FATHER$_R$ of" is an intransitive relation. So, it is an irreflexive one.

(b) "Being GREATER$_R$ than" is a transitive relation. It is also irreflexive. So, it is asymmetrical.

(c) "Logical EQUIVALENCE"$_R$ is a transitive relation. It is also symmetrical. So, it is reflexive.

230. (CHALLENGING) A student of mine, Paul Kaufman, devised his own version of the "Liar Paradox." The paradox involves a Cretan, Epimenides, who announced 'Cretans never tell the truth'. For ease of reference we name Epimenides' statement *George*. Kaufman's formulation of the paradox:

Epimenides SAID$_R$ George. Epimenides is a CRETAN. George is TRUE iff Cretans never say what is true. Hence, George is true iff it is not true.

Either establish the validity of this argument by formal proof or demonstrate its invalidity by the method of interpretation.

231. (CHALLENGING) Construct proofs for the valid arguments and interpretations for the others.

(a) (x)(y)(Rxy → Sxy) ⊢ (x)(y) [Rxy → (Sxy & Syx)]

(b) (x)(y) [(Fx & Fy) → Sxy] ⊢ (x)(y) [(Fx & Fy) → (Sxy & Syx)]

(c) (x)(y)(Rxy → Ryx) ⊢ (x)(y)(Rxy ↔ Ryx)

(d) (∃x)(∃y)(Rxy → Ryx) ⊢ (∃x)(∃y)(Rxy ↔ Ryx)

(e) "R" is transitive. It is symmetrical. So, it is totally reflexive.

(f) "R" is asymmetrical. So, it is not symmetrical.

232. (CHALLENGING) Establish the validity or invalidity of this argument.

Every VALID wff in NORMAL form is DERIVABLE. Any wff either is in normal form or is REDUCIBLE$_R$ to some wff in normal form. A wff which is reducible to a derivable wff in normal form is itself derivable. Therefore, every valid wff is derivable.

(UD: wffs)

chapter twelve

Natural Arguments

12.1
Introduction

In the preceding chapters I have tried to show (by providing examples) that arguments occur in all media involving language – in books and newspapers, lectures and casual conversations, movies and television broadcasts, and so on. I call such arguments "natural arguments" and contrast them with the "artificial arguments" which populate the exercise sets of many logic textbooks. In the present chapter I discuss the procedures involved in assessing natural arguments. I hope that your ability to assess natural predicate arguments has been strengthened by your study of earlier chapters and that it will be further increased by your study of this chapter. The twenty-two natural-argument passages at the end of the chapter will help you gauge your proficiency in this area.

The first step in the process of assessing a natural argument is to *identify* it as an argument. I assume that by this stage in your study of logic you have developed the knack of spotting arguments. For a discussion of argument identification, see section 14.1 of my *Introduction to Logic: Propositional Logic.*
When an argument has been located, the second step in its analysis

can be taken: *formalization*. Natural arguments are not usually cast in "standard form"—they may contain extraneous material and very often essential elements are left unstated. By "formalization" I mean the process of restating the argument in a purified or regularized form, a form in which all essential parts are made explicit and all nonessentials are eliminated.

After an argument has been formalized, a judgment must be made about the branch of logic most suitable for its assessment. Most natural deductive arguments may be assessed in one or both of these branches of logic: propositional logic and predicate logic. A few natural deductive arguments are best handled in some third area of logic. If you encounter a natural argument of this sort (which is unlikely), then at this point in your study of logic you will be forced to rely upon your native logical intuition in evaluating it.

Symbolization is the next step in the process of assessing a natural argument. If the argument will be treated in predicate logic, an appropriate UD must be selected and letters chosen to abbreviate predicates and singular terms. If propositional logic is being employed, then, of course, no UD is involved, but capital letters will be selected to abbreviate simple statements. After the UD and the symbols have been chosen, the argument may be symbolized.

When a natural argument has been symbolized, its *form can be evaluated*. If the argument is being assessed in predicate logic, one or more of the three techniques explained in this book will be appropriate: proofs, diagrams, and interpretations. If the argument is treated in propositional logic, one or both of these methods will apply: proofs and truth tables.[1] In determining which logical test to employ, it will often be necessary to make a preliminary "educated guess" about the validity (invalidity) of the argument under examination.

If the argument under study should prove to be valid, it does *not* follow that the argument establishes the truth of its conclusion. A valid argument proves its conclusion iff all its premises are true. I label the task of judging the truth of the premises of an argument *evaluating its content*. This is a crucial step in the assessment of an argument, but it has been ignored in the text for an obvious reason. Because an argument can have any subject matter whatever, no one textbook or single college course could prepare you for the task of evaluating content. Furthermore, unless the subject matter of the argument under assessment is logic, a logician will probably not be in a good position either to judge its content or to teach others how to judge its content. For example, the *content* of an argument about the spawning habits of salmon can be assessed intelligently by an icthyologist or (perhaps) by a fisherman, but not by a logician (unless he happens also to be an icthyologist or fisherman). Your ability to assess correctly the *form* of arguments should be improved by your study of formal logic. Your capacity to judge accurately

---

[1] For a discussion of truth tables, see Chapters Ten and Eleven of *Introduction to Logic: Propositional Logic*.

the *content* of arguments should be increased by your entire education (both in and out of schools).

I have analyzed the process of assessing natural arguments into six steps:

    (1)   identification

    (2)   formalization

    (3)   determination of appropriate branch of logic

    (4)   symbolization

    (5)   evaluation of form

    (6)   evaluation of content

The assessment of an argument will not always proceed exactly on this schedule. Sometimes when one is working on stage (4) or stage (5) it will become obvious that the formalization of the argument needs to be altered, or that the wrong branch of logic was selected. When such a discovery is made, one must backtrack to stage (2) or (3). On occasion one will discover while at stage (5) that the argument has been improperly symbolized. In this situation, also, retracing is required. Some of these back-and-forth processes are illustrated in section 12.2. Note that when the logical technique employed in stage (5) is diagrams, stage (4) is unnecessary.

Many natural arguments were presented by direct quotation in the text and exercise sets of preceding chapters. Usually I formalized such arguments for you, and in all cases I selected the UD and picked the abbreviating letters. In most cases I also chose the logical technique to be used in evaluating the form of the argument. The point is that you have had little or no practice in making decisions of these kinds. I devote the remainder of the chapter to a discussion of such decisions. My plan will be to provide a detailed assessment of five natural arguments, explaining my choices and decisions as I make them. I hope that you will then be in a position to make similar choices intelligently as you work through the natural arguments collected at the end of the chapter.

12.2
Examples

(EXAMPLE ONE: THE CHAMELEON) Upon spotting a chameleon on our patio wall, my son Mark (aged four) remarked:

> *He's a live one, isn't he? — 'cause he moves!*

My first attempt at formalizing this argument yields:

> The chameleon on the wall moves.
> So, it is alive.

It is clear that an important element is missing from the argument as so far set forth. An argument with a missing or unstated element (or elements) is called an *enthymeme*. Most natural arguments are enthymematic. The missing part or parts may be premises or the conclusion or both. It is obvious that unstated elements must be made explicit before the analysis of an argument can proceed further. What is missing from the "chameleon" argument is a premise which asserts a connection between movement and life. Here are two distinct formulations of that premise:

> If the chameleon on the wall moves, then it is alive.
>
> All moving chameleons are alive.

It is impossible at this date to determine which of these statements (if either) Mark had in mind. Which should be added to the argument? In some cases where there are two distinct formulations of some suppressed element, there are good reasons for preferring one. In this instance, however, the two versions of the missing premise seem equally acceptable to me. Let's examine both formalizations of the "chameleon" argument which result from the inclusion of the two versions of this premise.

When we incorporate the conditional premise this formalization results:

> The chameleon on the wall moves.
>
> If it moves, then it is alive.
>
> So, it is alive.

This argument belongs to propositional logic. Two facts which point in this direction: (1) the argument contains no *general* statements, and (2) it does contain a *compound* statement (specifically, a conditional). Either of these facts by itself would suggest propositional-logic treatment; the two combined provide strong evidence.

Because of the simplicity of the argument's form *(modus ponens)*, we can tell at a glance that it is valid. One might be inclined in this instance to skip the fourth step: symbolization. However, for purposes of illustration, let's take that step. We must devise a "dictionary"—that is, select capitals and indicate the simple statements they abbreviate.

> M = The chameleon on the wall moves
> A = The chameleon on the wall is alive

The argument is readily symbolized:

> M, M → A ⊢ A

The validity of this symbolized argument may be demonstrated by formal-proof or truth-table techniques.

If we incorporate into the argument the other version of the missing premise, we get this formalization:

> The chameleon on the wall moves.
>
> All moving chameleons are alive.
>
> So, the chameleon on the wall is alive.

This argument requires treatment in predicate logic. Two facts about the argument suggest this: (1) there is at least one general statement (the second premise), and (2) there are no compound statements.

The next stage in our analysis is symbolization, and at this point we must select a universe of discourse. As each statement in the argument treats only chameleons, it is permissible to employ "chameleons" as the UD. A dictionary is required. The formalization contains one singular term ('the chameleon on the wall') and three predicates, but one of the predicates ('is a chameleon') is not assigned an abbreviation because it corresponds to the UD adopted. I choose this dictionary:

$$w = \text{the chameleon on the wall}$$
$$Mx = x \text{ moves}$$
$$Ax = x \text{ is alive}$$

The argument is symbolized:

$$Mw, (x)(Mx \rightarrow Ax) \vdash Aw$$

The validity of this symbolized argument can be demonstrated by constructing a formal proof. Of course, the argument's validity can also be established by diagram.

Perhaps more should be said about the selection of a UD. By the "standard UD" I mean the class of everything (or, more properly, the class of everything except classes). By a "restricted UD" I mean any UD smaller than the standard one. It is always correct to employ the standard UD in analyzing a predicate argument. For a given predicate argument, some restricted UD's will be appropriate and others will not. The following principle offers a criterion for determining the appropriateness of a restricted UD:

> **A class, X, is an acceptable UD for a given predicate argument iff (1) each statement in the argument treats *only* individuals belonging to X and (2) X has at least one member.**

By applying this principle we can determine that "chameleons," "reptiles," and "animals" are all appropriate UD's for the "chameleon" argument. We can also discover with the help of this principle that "female chameleons" and "things on walls" are inappropriate UD's.

When symbolizing a predicate argument we ordinarily have a choice between adopting the standard UD or a restricted UD; often several restricted UD's will be appropriate. Suppose all the statements in some argument treat only red-headed Lutherans. In symbolizing this argument we can choose from among these UD's:

> everything
>
> people
>
> Lutherans
>
> red-headed people
>
> red-headed Lutherans

Are there grounds for preferring one of these UD's to another? In general, if one UD permits a simpler symbolization than a second UD, the former is to be preferred. A simpler symbolization is desirable for its own sake and because it may simplify or shorten the process of testing for validity. A more restricted or smaller UD will often result in a simpler symbolization. Adopting "red-headed Lutherans" as a UD eliminates predicate letters abbreviating 'is red-headed' and 'is Lutheran'.

I mentioned above that the standard UD can always be chosen. When that UD is selected for the "chameleon" argument, we reach initially the following symbolization:

The chameleon on the wall moves.	Mw
All moving chameleons are alive.	(x) [(Mx & Cx) → Ax]
So, the chameleon on the wall is alive.	⊢ Aw

($Cx = x$ is a chameleon) However, this symbolized argument is invalid, as you can easily establish. What is missing from the symbolization is a formula which asserts that individual w is a chameleon. This formula may be added as an extra premise or it may be conjoined to the first symbolized premise. The latter choice yields this symbolization of the argument:

Mw & Cw, (x) [(Mx & Cx) → Ax] ⊢ Aw

Translating the symbolized first premise into English we reach:

The chameleon on the wall is a moving chameleon.

The redundancy may be removed by allowing the name w to abbreviate 'the animal on the wall' (rather than 'the chameleon on the wall'). This involves modifying the formalization of the argument to:

> The animal on the wall is a moving chameleon.
>
> All moving chameleons are alive.
>
> So, the animal on the wall is alive.

Symbolizing the argument has led to an alteration of the English formalization; this is not uncommon.

(EXAMPLE TWO: LIZA MINNELLI) Another example is provided by this portion of a gossip column:

> Q: *Desi Arnaz, Jr., fathered a child with Patty Duke. Didn't he also father a child with Liza Minnelli?*
>
> —*Mrs. E. B., Elmont, N.Y.*
>
> A: *Impossible. Liza (with a "z") has never been a mother.*[2]

When irrelevant matters (such as the business about Patty Duke) are dropped, this tentative formalization of the argument emerges:

> Liza Minnelli is not a mother.
>
> Thus, Desi Arnaz, Jr., did not father a child with Liza.

This can be transformed into a valid propositional argument by introducing a conditional premise:

> If Desi fathered a child with Liza, then Liza is a mother.

The resulting formalization exhibits the *modus tollens* pattern. While the "Liza" argument may be handled in this manner, I think it is preferable to treat it as a predicate argument. When we view it as a predicate argument, we need not add any suppressed premises. As a general principle, if the validity of an argument is preserved in one treatment without the addition of extra premises while under a second treatment additional premises are required, the first treatment does a better job of revealing the logical structure of the argument.

A UD of "people" will be appropriate for the predicate-logic symbolization of this argument. There remains a question about which symbols to select and specifically whether the predicate letters should be regarded as abbreviating one-, two-, or three-place predicates. This is a question about the *depth* to which the analysis of the argument should be carried. Here are three symbolizations which involve analyses carried to different levels:

---

[2] From *Glad You Asked That*, by Marilyn and Hy Gardner, courtesy of Field Newspaper Syndicate. *Miami News*, July 24, 1973, p. 8-B.

PROPERTY ANALYSIS	$\sim(\exists x)Lx \vdash \sim(\exists x)(Dx\ \&\ Lx)$ Lx = Liza is mother of x Dx = Desi is father of x
DYADIC RELATIONAL ANALYSIS	$\sim(\exists x)Mlx \vdash \sim(\exists x)(Fdx\ \&\ Mlx)$ $Mxy = x$ is mother of y l = Liza $Fxy = x$ is father of y d = Desi
TRIADIC RELATIONAL ANALYSIS	$\sim(\exists x)(\exists y)Fxyl \vdash \sim(\exists x)Fdxl$ $Fxyz = x$ fathers y with z l = Liza d = Desi

These three symbolized arguments are valid. I regard all three as acceptable symbolizations. Simplicity seems the only relevant respect in which they can be contrasted. On this ground I would prefer the first symbolization (the property analysis) if pressed for a decision. The "Liza" argument is unusual in that it can be symbolized on so many different levels.

(EXAMPLE THREE: TED HENDRICKS) A sports story starts:

> *Ted Hendricks began wondering which National Football League team he'd be traded to as soon as he signed a 1975 contract with the Jacksonville Sharks of the World Football League. The former University of Miami standout knew he was through in Baltimore after five seasons.*
> *"I anticipated a trade, seeing as one of [Colts general manager] Joe Thomas' favorite quotes is nobody plays out his option in Baltimore," Hendricks said.*[3]

Hendricks is advancing an argument whose conclusion is that he will be traded by the Colts. The argument may be given this formal exposition:

No Baltimore Colt plays out his option.

Ted Hendricks is a Colt.

Unless Hendricks is traded he will play out his option.

Therefore, Hendricks will be traded.

---

[3] Charlie Nobles, "Hendricks Happy to Get Visiting Rights," *Miami News*, August 27, 1974, p. 1-C.

The third premise in the formalization was not stated explicitly in the newspaper story, but it obviously was assumed.

Is this argument best treated in propositional or predicate logic? There are conflicting indicators. The third premise is a compound statement—a fact which suggests a propositional analysis. Another premise (the first) is a general statement—a feature which indicates a predicate analysis. In a situation such as this, one might attempt both treatments, and then determine which is better. A propositional symbolization:

$\sim$P, C, $\sim$T $\to$ O $\vdash$ T

P = Some Colts play out their options

C = Hendricks is a Colt

T = Hendricks will be traded

O = Hendricks plays out his option

In this symbolization, no connection is shown between the first premise and any other statement in the argument, and none is shown between the second premise and the remaining statements. In the English formalization the first premise has something in common with the second (the predicate 'is a Colt') and something in common with the third (the predicate 'plays out his option'). The propositional symbolization does not reveal important logical features of the argument. The propositional symbolization is invalid, yet the English argument seems valid (even without the addition of auxiliary premises). All of this suggests the inadequacy of a propositional treatment and leads me to try a predicate analysis.

Adopting a UD of "people," I devise this predicate symbolization:

(x)(Cx $\to$ $\sim$Px), Ch, $\sim$Th $\to$ Ph $\vdash$ Th

$Cx = x$ is a Colt

$Px = x$ plays out x's option

h = Hendricks

$Tx = x$ will be traded

The validity of this symbolization can be shown by formal proof. Diagrams are inapplicable because the conditional third premise cannot be diagramed.

The statement 'Ted Hendricks will be traded' occurs in the third premise and the conclusion. While this statement was symbolized above with a wff from predicate logic ('Th'), the validity of the argument does not require that the analysis of the statement be carried this far. If the statement were treated as an unanalyzed simple statement, the validity of the argument would still be demonstrable. This fact suggests the following symbolization of the argument:

(x)(Cx $\to$ $\sim$Px), Ch, $\sim$T $\to$ Ph $\vdash$ T

In this symbolization *T* abbreviates the statement 'Ted Hendricks will be traded' in the manner of propositional logic. The symbolized argument represents a fusion of both branches of logic. In order to prevent confusion, I have avoided such hybrid symbolizations in preceding chapters of the book; they are, however, perfectly legitimate. You may find it desirable to produce hybrid symbolizations of one or two arguments in the exercise set following this chapter. The techniques of formal proof and interpretation apply to hybrid symbolizations; the methods of diagrams and truth tables do not. When the method of interpretation is applied to a hybrid argument, each statement letter must be interpreted with a statement.

(EXAMPLE FOUR: THE SHANTY) An excerpt from Laura Ingalls Wilder's biography *The Long Winter:*

> "We've got to wait for the train," Pa said. *"We can't move to the claim till it comes."*
> Tightly as he had nailed and battened the tar-paper to the shanty, blizzard winds had torn it loose and whipped it to shreds, letting in the snow at sides and roof. And now the spring rains were beating in through the cracks. *The shanty must be repaired before anyone could live in it and Pa could not repair it until the train came,* for there was no tar-paper at the lumberyard.[4]

This passage contains an argument whose conclusion is the claim that the (Ingalls) family cannot move into the claim shanty until the train arrives. The purpose of the argument is not to prove the conclusion but to *explain* it; the argument is an explanation. Concentrating on the parts of the passage I have italicized, I produce this preliminary formalization:

> The shanty will be repaired before the Ingalls move into it.
>
> The shanty will not be repaired until the train comes.
>
> So, the Ingalls won't move into the shanty until the train comes.

Other formalizations of the argument are possible; here is a more complex version:

> The shanty will be repaired before the Ingalls move into it.
>
> The shanty will not be repaired until Pa buys tar-paper.
>
> Pa will not buy tar-paper until there is tar-paper at the lumberyard.
>
> There will be no tar-paper at the lumberyard until the train comes.
>
> So, the Ingalls won't move into the shanty until the train comes.

Both of these formalizations are legitimate interpretations of the argument presented in the passage, and there are still other acceptable in-

[4](New York: Harper & Row, Publishers, 1940, 1953), p. 314. Italics added.

terpretations. (It does *not* follow, of course, that just *any* interpretation is adequate.) I arbitrarily select the first formalization provided.

Noting the terms 'before' and 'until' in the formalization, I decide that the argument involves the relation of "occurring before" (temporal priority) and that the appropriate UD will be "moments of time." Having chosen this UD, I attempt to phrase each predicate in terms of moments of time. These symbols are selected:

> Rx = the shanty is repaired at time x
> Bxy = time x is before time y
> Mx = the Ingalls move into the shanty at time x
> Tx = the train comes at time x

Formula F2 was my first attempted symbolization of premise one (S1).

> (S1)   The shanty will be repaired before the Ingalls move into it.
> (F2)   (x)(y) [(Rx & My) → Bxy]

For some time I believed that F2 was an accurate symbolization; then I discovered that F2 is logically equivalent to F3, which symbolizes S3.

> (F3)   (x)~Rx ∨ (x)(y) [(Rx & My) → Bxy]
> (S3)   Either the shanty is never repaired or else it is repaired before the Ingalls move into it.

You can dispel any doubts about the logical equivalence of F2 and F3 by constructing two formal proofs. It is obvious that S1 and S3 have different content;[5] hence F2 is not an acceptable symbolization of S1. The real difficulty with F2 is that it lacks the existential implications of S1. Even when coupled with the assertion that there was a time when the family moved into the shanty, F2 does not imply that there was a time when the shanty was repaired. This problem is overcome by F1, which is a correct symbolization of S1.

> (F1)   (x) [Mx → (∃y)(Ry & Byx)]

How did I discover the inadequacy of F2? By attempting to construct a proof for my symbolization (which included F2). After some initial failures to complete the proof, I realized that a premise was required which asserted that there was a time when the shanty was repaired. At first I planned to add such a premise to my formalization of the argument, but more thought convinced me that the root of the problem was my symbolization of S1. When S1 was properly symbolized, the extra existential

---

[5] To grasp the difference in content, note that the following statement is consistent with S3 but inconsistent with S1.

Although the shanty was never repaired the Ingalls did move into it.

premise proved unneeded and was eliminated. This experience of learning something about the proper symbolization of an argument while attempting to construct a proof is a common one.

Eventually I reached this symbolization of my formalization of the argument:

The shanty will be repaired before the Ingalls move into it.
$$(x) [Mx \rightarrow (\exists y)(Ry \ \& \ Byx)]$$

The shanty will not be repaired until the train comes.
$$(x) [Rx \rightarrow (\exists y)(Ty \ \& \ {\sim}Bxy)]$$

So, the Ingalls won't move into the shanty until the train comes.
$$\vdash (x) [Mx \rightarrow (\exists y)(Ty \ \& \ {\sim}Bxy)]$$

I was quite confident of the correctness of this symbolization, but the proof continued to elude me. I realized that one or more auxiliary premises enunciating the logical features of the relation of "occurring before" were required to complete the argument. My first guess was that the argument involved the transitivity of this relation; this guess proved correct. When I added the following wff to the premise set of the symbolized argument, I was able to finish the proof.

$$(x)(y)(z) [(Bxy \ \& \ Byz) \rightarrow Bxz]$$

Had I remained unsuccessful at this point, I next would have added a premise asserting the asymmetry of the relation. Missing premises are often discovered when initial proof attempts fail. One is especially motivated to search for auxiliary premises when (as in the present case) one is convinced of the validity of an argument but nevertheless cannot complete the proof.

Through the use of formal logic in assessing arguments one's understanding of the logical structure of arguments is often increased. The "shanty" argument is an example. When I first encountered that argument, I judged it to be valid, but there was much about the argument that I did not grasp. For example, I had a hunch that the argument presupposed the transitivity of the relation "occurring before," but I was not confident about the matter. I had no idea whether the argument presupposed the asymmetry or irreflexivity of this relation. By the time I finished applying the methods of symbolic logic to the argument, I was clear about each of these points. In these and other ways my understanding of the structure of the argument had been aided by the technology of symbolic logic.

(EXAMPLE FIVE: GEOMETRY) During a philosophy lecture I attended the speaker remarked, "No primitive man can do geometry." A friend (call him 'Al') sitting by me whispered, "Hell, *I* can't do geometry!

Does that make me primitive?" It was clear from his tone of voice that Al thought he had refuted the speaker. I understood Al to be advancing an argument whose (unstated) conclusion is the negation of the speaker's comment. I formalized the argument this way:

> Al can't do geometry.
> Al is not primitive.
> Hence, it is false that no primitive person can do geometry.

Selecting a UD of people, I produced this symbolization:

$$\sim Ga, \ \sim Pa \vdash \sim(x)(Px \rightarrow \sim Gx)$$

$Gx = x$ can do geometry

$a = $ Al

$Px = x$ is primitive

Both the method of diagrams and the method of interpretation will establish the invalidity of my formalization of the "geometry" argument.

Have I shown that *Al* was making a logical mistake—that *his* argument (as distinct from *my* formalization) is invalid? Perhaps (it could be suggested) he was employing some unstated premise(s) which in combination with his stated premises entails the conclusion. Notice that any invalid argument can be transformed into a valid one by the addition of suitably strong auxiliary premises. This thought raises an interesting question: what criteria govern the (legitimate) addition of premises to an argument under investigation? If there are no such criteria, then any (apparently) invalid argument may be changed into a valid one. This would support the absurd thesis that no one ever advances an invalid argument. I propose these criteria:

> **An unstated premise may be added to an argument iff**
> **(1) it is logically true or true by definition, or**
> **(2) it is recognized to be true by everyone, or**
> **(3) it would be accepted as true by the arguer.**

I suggest that it is legitimate to include in an argument a relevant premise which satisfies any one of these criteria and incorrect to add a premise which satisfies none of them. It is particularly important that relevant auxiliary premises be added to arguments we judge to be invalid, for otherwise our judgment of invalidity *may* result from a failure to include a premise that the arguer was assuming but not stating. The total argument may be valid although the exposed portion is not. Some arguments will remain invalid even after every relevant additional premise satisfying one of my proposed criteria has been included. When this is the case you can confidently assess the argument as invalid.

Returning to the "geometry" argument: a little thought should convince you that no auxiliary premises satisfying any of the criteria listed above will transform it into a valid inference. Al can justly be accused of logical sin. The speaker had claimed that primitiveness is a sufficient condition of geometrical ignorance. Al's whispered comments refute a quite different claim, that geometrical ignorance is a sufficient condition of primitiveness. His transgression was to confuse these claims. A better grounding in logic might have enabled Al to avoid the mistake.

In assessing the natural arguments at the end of the chapter I found it necessary to add suppressed elements (premises and/or the conclusion) in about half the cases. Your treatments, of course, may differ legitimately from mine.

12.3
Postscript

It is quite likely that one year from the day you close this book for the final time you will have forgotten the restrictions on the EO Rule and will be unable to symbolize complex relational sentences. In spite of this, I believe the book will have been a success if as a result of working through it you are more aware of the natural arguments you encounter, more likely to question the form and content of such arguments, more inclined to back up your assertions with arguments, and more prone to expect others to support their questionable claims with reasons.

If I have been fortunate enough to whet your appetite for further logic study, you might read some of the books listed below. Copi's text provides a more advanced treatment of (propositional and) predicate logic. Hunter discusses theoretical questions about formal systems of logic. The Kneales' book is a comprehensive history of deductive logic. Iseminger has collected 21 essays on philosophical issues which arise in the study of logic. For additional references see the several essays on logic at the end of volume four and the beginning of volume five of *The Encyclopedia of Philosophy* (New York: Macmillan Publishing Co., Inc., 1967).

Irving M. Copi, *Symbolic Logic* (4th ed.). New York: The Macmillan Company, 1973.

Geoffrey Hunter, *Metalogic: An Introduction to the Metatheory of Standard First Order Logic.* Berkeley and Los, Angeles: University of California Press, 1971.

William and Martha Kneale, *The Development of Logic.* Oxford: The Clarendon Press, 1962.

Gary Iseminger, ed., *Logic and Philosophy: Selected Readings.* New York: Appleton-Century-Crofts, 1968.

EXERCISES

Instructions for exercises 112 through 133 (and 233–238): Each passage contains an argument. (1) Formalize the argument, taking care to supply any suppressed elements. (2) Decide whether the argument should be treated in predicate logic or propositional logic. (Only a few are best treated as propositional.) (3) Select a UD (for predicate arguments) and choose abbreviating symbols, then symbolize the argument. (4) Make an intuitive assessment of validity; then either demonstrate validity by formal proof or diagram, or establish invalidity by interpretation, diagram or (for a propositional argument) truth table.

112. "There is a large difference between giving a motive or reason for an action and trying to state its cause. Motives are not the right sort of things to be causes, because they are not events or happenings. Something can be classified as a cause only if it is an event. . . ."

> Fred A. Westphal, *The Activity of Philosophy*
> (Englewood Cliffs, N.J.: Prentice-Hall, Inc.,
> 1969), p. 158.

113. Campus conversation:
    HISTORY TEACHER: "Is it true that every member of the philosophy department knows the salary of every member of the department?"
    PHILOSOPHY TEACHER (POSPESEL): "No. There are members of the department whose salary I don't know."

114. "Have you ever noticed that every person who thinks she is beautiful is always looking in a mirror. My roommate thinks she is beautiful. I know because she is constantly looking at herself in mirrors."

> Letter from University of Illinois coed to
> University of Miami student, Stephanie Kazarian, December 5, 1972.

115. "We like the beautiful and don't like the ugly; therefore, what we like is beautiful, and what we don't like is ugly. . . ."

> Charles Ives, *Essays before a Sonata, The Majority, and other Writings*, ed. by Howard Boatwright (New York: W. W. Norton & Co., Inc., 1962), p. 77.

116. "Most religious groups condemn . . . euthanasia. The Roman Catholic view is that euthanasia without the patient's consent is murder, and with his consent, suicide."

> Joyce Brothers, "The 'Good Death' Controversy,"
> *Miami News*, May 9, 1974, p. 7-B.

117. "After the ladies were gone, we talked of the Highlanders' not having sheets; and so on we went to the advantage of wearing linen. Mr. Johnson said, 'All animal substances are less cleanly than vegetable. Wool, of which

flannel is made, is an animal substance; flannel therefore is not so cleanly as linen.'"

> James Boswell, *The Life of Samuel Johnson* in *The Portable Johnson & Boswell* (New York: The Viking Press, Inc., 1947), p. 401.

118. "STOIC: . . . I can turn you into a stone right now if I like.
"BUYER: A stone? My dear chap, you aren't Perseus.
"STOIC: Just you listen. Is a stone a substance?
"BUYER: Yes.
"STOIC: Isn't an animate being a substance?
"BUYER: Yes.
"STOIC: And you're an animate being?
"BUYER: I suppose so.
"STOIC: Then you're a substance, so you're a stone."

> Lucian, *The Sale of Philosophers* in *Selected Works* (Indianapolis: The Bobbs-Merrill Company, Inc., 1965), pp. 107–108.

119. "Gale Sayers is too blunt to make it as a network television announcer. Just before halftime in last week's WFL game, Sayers, working as guest announcer, pointed out, 'Detroit has got to stop this drive, or they're out of the game.' Detroit didn't stop the drive, Chicago took a 28–8 lead and it must be presumed that channels were switched all over America."

> John Crittenden, "Ali-Foreman on TV: $20, but it'll Sell," *Miami News*, August 27, 1974, p. 2-C.

120.

> January 22, 1970. By permission of John Hart and Field Enterprises, Inc.

121. "The set of real numbers greater than 0 but less than or equal to 1 is a subset of the set of real numbers. We have just shown that it is uncountable. By 13.1 any subset of a countable set is countable. So the set of (all) real numbers is uncountable. Q.E.D."

Geoffrey Hunter, *Metalogic: An Introduction to the Metatheory of Stand-*

ard First Order Logic (Berkeley and Los Angeles: University of California Press, 1971), p. 32.

122. "The indeterminist believes that no caused acts are free, that some human acts are uncaused, and hence, some human acts are free."

From a midterm examination in Introduction to Philosophy, University of Miami, April 4, 1975.

123. "A cause must be temporally prior to its effect. No cause follows its effect. If each cause were contemporary with its effect, then all events would be simultaneous. But this is patently absurd. So, a cause must be temporally prior to its effect."

Philosophy master's thesis, rough draft.

124. "YONKERS, N.Y.—A 54-year-old Roman Catholic physician has resigned as chief of obstetrics at Yonkers General Hospital because he couldn't reconcile his religious views with the state's liberalized abortion law.

"Dr. Robert R. Onorato, father of seven, said: 'I feel it is morally wrong to take a human life.' He added that he thought interrupting a pregnancy, at whatever stage, amounted to taking life."

"Physician Quits over Abortions," *Miami News*, July 4, 1970, p. 4-A.

125. "The best argument against considering the unusual features of the avian respiratory system [air sacs and pneumatized bones] as being necessary for flight is provided by bats. They have typical mammalian lungs and do not have air sacs or pneumatized bones, and yet they are excellent fliers."

Knut Schmidt-Nielsen, "How Birds Breathe," *Scientific American*, December, 1971, p. 74.

126. "Cigarets are like women—the best ones are thin and rich. Silva Thins are thin and rich."

Television commercial.

127. "WASHINGTON—Idaho's Snake River Canyon, where every prospect pleases and only man is vile, soon will be the scene of a remarkable example of man's work. On Sept. 8, Evel Knievel will try to leap 1,500 feet across the canyon on a 350 mph motorcycle. . . .

"He estimates that he has a 50-50 chance of failing in his jump, and falling to his death in the canyon. If the jump is not as risky as it is advertised to be, it is a fraud. If, as seems probable, it does involve serious risk of Knievel's death, it is obscene."

George Will, "Evel Knievel's up to no Good" (Washington Post), *Miami News*, September 2, 1974, p. 9-A.

128. "One day when dining at old Mr. Langton's, where Miss Roberts, his niece, was one of the company, Johnson, with his usual complacent attention to the fair sex, took her by the hand and said, 'My dear, I hope you are a Ja-

cobite.' Old Mr. Langton, who, though a high and steady Tory, was attached to the present Royal Family, seemed offended, and asked Johnson, with great warmth [i.e., heat], what he could mean by putting such a question to his niece! 'Why, Sir, (said Johnson) I meant no offence to your niece, I meant her a great compliment. A Jacobite, Sir, believes in the divine right of Kings. He that believes in the divine right of Kings believes in a Divinity. A Jacobite believes in the divine right of Bishops. He that believes in the divine right of Bishops believes in the divine authority of the Christian religion. Therefore Sir, a Jacobite is neither an Atheist nor a Deist.'"

James Boswell, *The Life of Samuel Johnson* in *The Portable Johnson & Boswell* (New York: The Viking Press, Inc., 1947), p. 107.

129. "Determinism is the view that all events are caused. 'All events are caused' becomes basically the notion that any event is so connected with some preceding event that unless the earlier event had occurred, the later event would not have occurred. Hence, given any event *A*, it is so connected with a later event *B*, that given *A*, *B* *must* occur."

Introduction-to-philosophy term paper.

130. "'[Soldat du Chêne is] one good Indian!' Pa said. No matter what Mr. Scott said, Pa did not believe that the only good Indian was a dead Indian."

Laura Ingalls Wilder, *Little House on the Prairie* (New York: Harper & Row, Publishers, 1935, 1953), p. 301.

131. "There is, therefore, a power of gravity tending to all the planets. . . . And since all attraction (by Law III) is mutual, Jupiter will therefore gravitate towards all his own satellites. . . ."

Isaac Newton, *Mathematical Principles of Natural Philosophy* (Berkeley: University of California Press, 1960). Book III, Proposition V, Corollary I, p. 410.

132.

July 3, 1970. By permission of John Hart and Field Enterprises, Inc.

133. "Every proposition is either true or false, and no proposition is both true and false. (Hence if something is neither true nor false, or is . . . both true and false, it is not to count as a proposition in the present context.)"

G. E. Hughes and M. J. Cresswell, *An Introduction to Modal Logic* (London: Methuen and Co., Ltd., 1968), p. 5.

233. (CHALLENGING) "A set A is a *subset* of a set B iff there is no member of A that is not a member of B. The empty set, $\emptyset$, is a subset of every set, since for any set C there is no member of $\emptyset$ that is not a member of C, simply because there is no member of $\emptyset$."

> Geoffrey Hunter, *Metalogic: An Introduction to the Metatheory of Standard First Order Logic* (Berkeley and Los Angeles: University of California Press, 1971), p. 21.

234. (CHALLENGING) "According to Behaviorist doctrine, mental events are behavioral events. . . . So mental events are always effects of whatever causes human behavior. . . ."

> Keith Campbell, *Body and Mind* (Garden City, N.Y.: Doubleday & Company, Inc., 1970), p. 65.

235. (CHALLENGING) "(8.21) *Special Consequence Condition.* If an observation report confirms a hypothesis *H*, then it also confirms every consequence of *H*.

"(8.22) *Equivalence Condition.* If an observation report confirms a hypothesis *H*, then it also confirms every hypothesis which is logically equivalent with *H*.

"This follows from (8.21) in view of the fact that equivalent hypotheses are mutual consequences of each other."

> Carl G. Hempel, "Studies in the Logic of Confirmation (II)," *Mind*, April, 1945, p. 103.

236. (CHALLENGING)

> Reprinted by permission of the Chicago Tribune-New York News Syndicate, Inc. Copyright 1974. All rights reserved.

237. (CHALLENGING) "AUGUSTINE: If, now, we could find something which you could unhesitatingly recognize not only as existing but also as superior to our reason, would you have any hesitation in calling it, whatever it may be, God?

"EVODIUS: Well, . . . I do not wish to say simply that God is that to which my reason is inferior, but that above which there is no superior.

"AUG.: Clearly so.

. . .

"AUG.: I promised, if you remember, to show you something superior to the human mind and reason. There it is, truth itself.

. . .

"AUG.: You admitted for your part that if I could show you something superior to our minds you would confess that it was God, provided nothing existed that was higher still. I accepted your admission and said it would be sufficient if I demonstrated that. If there is anything more excellent than wisdom [i.e., truth], doubtless it, rather, is God. But if there is nothing more excellent, then truth itself is God. Whether there is or is not such a higher thing, you cannot deny that God exists, and this was the question set for our discussion."

Augustine, "On Free Will," Book II, Chs. 6, 13 & 15 in
Augustine: Earlier Writings, trans. by John H. S. Burleigh
(Philadelphia: The Westminster Press, 1953), pp. 144, 157 & 159.

238. (CHALLENGING) ". . . [The astronomer] Apelles says that the spots seen in the sun are much blacker than any of those ever observed in the moon. This I believe to be absolutely false; I hold, on the contrary, that the sunspots are at least as bright as the brightest part of the moon, and my reasoning is as follows. When Venus appears as evening star it is very splendid; yet it is not seen until many degrees distant from the sun, particularly if both are well above the horizon. This is because the regions of the sky around the sun are no less bright than Venus itself. From this we may deduce that if we could place the full moon directly beside the sun, it would remain quite invisible, being situated in a field no less bright than itself. Now consider the fact that when we look at the brilliant solar disk through the telescope, it appears much brighter than the field which surrounds it; and then let us compare the blackness of the sunspots both with the sun's own light and with the darkness of the adjacent surroundings. From the two comparisons we shall find that the sunspots are no darker than the field surrounding the sun. Now if this is so, and if the moon itself would remain imperceptible in the brightness of those same surroundings, then we are forced to the conclusion that the sunspots are not a bit less bright than the shining parts of the moon—even though, situated as they are in the very brilliant field of the sun's disk, they look cloudy and black to us. And if they yield nothing in brightness to the lightest parts of the moon, what will they be in comparison with the moon's darkest spots?"

Galileo Galilei, "First Letter to Mark Welser concerning the Solar Spots, May 4, 1612" in *Discoveries and Opinions of Galileo,* trans. by Stillman Drake (Garden City, N.Y.: Doubleday & Company, Inc., 1957), pp. 92–93.

239. (CHALLENGING) Locate in newspapers, magazines, books (other than logic texts), films, television broadcasts, or radio broadcasts five natural arguments which fall within the scope of predicate logic. For each argument provide (1) an accurate quotation of the argument in its original form;[6] (2) a reference to the source (title, date, page number, and so on); (3) your formalization of the argument (with needed suppressed elements supplied); (4) a symbolization, of your formalization (including a "dictionary" which indicates for each letter the predicate or singular term it abbreviates); and (5) an assessment of the argument which employs some technique explained in this book.

[6] Consider clipping or Xeroxing long passages.

appendix one

Propositional Logic: A Brief Review

Propositional logic treats the five connective expressions *not, and, or, if . . . then,* and *if and only if (iff).* The symbolic abbreviations of these connectives which are employed in this book are listed in the table below.

Propositional Connectives

ENGLISH CONNECTIVE	SYMBOL	SYMBOL NAME
not	~	tilde
and	&	ampersand
or	∨	wedge
if . . . then	→	arrow
if and only if	↔	double arrow

Simple statements (statements having no parts which are themselves statements) are abbreviated by capital letters. When a wff (well-formed formula) contains several connectives, their *scopes* are shown by groupers: parentheses, brackets, and braces. In the formula below, for example, the scope of the ampersand is limited by the parentheses and the scope of the arrow by the brackets; the entire wff falls within the scope of the tilde.

$$\sim [A \rightarrow (B \,\&\, C)]$$

Among the techniques for establishing the validity of propositional arguments, the method of formal proofs is of special importance. (An extension of this technique is used throughout this book.) Roughly, a formal proof (or simply "proof") of the validity of an argument is a list of statements with the premises of the argument at the top and the conclusion at the bottom. Each statement in the list is either an assumption or is deduced from statements above it by a stated rule of inference. Finally, every assumption on which the conclusion depends is a premise of the argument. Completing the proof establishes the validity of the argument.

There are many sets of inference rules for proofs in propositional logic. The set employed in this volume consists of eighteen rules. Ten of these rules are regarded as "primitive." There are two primitive rules for each connective: a rule which sanctions a move *to* a wff containing that connective (an "In" rule) and one which sanctions a move *from* a wff containing that connective (an "Out" rule). These ten rules are listed in the chart on page 203. The primitive rules constitute a *complete* set; that is, a proof which employs *only* these ten rules can be constructed for any valid propositional argument.

The remaining eight rules in our set of propositional inference rules are known as "derived" rules. They are derived in the sense that they can be validated by appeal to the primitive rules. The derived rules are listed in the chart on page 204. Each of the eighteen rules will be applied to *whole* lines but not to *parts* of lines.

Formal proofs in our formulation of propositional logic may be divided into two groups. In the first group are proofs which do not use any of the following four inference rules: Arrow In, Tilde In, Tilde Out, and Wedge Out. The format for these proofs consists of three columns: (1) line number, (2) statement, and (3) justification. I illustrate with a proof for this symbolized argument:

$$\sim D \lor E, \sim D \rightarrow \sim E \vdash D \leftrightarrow E$$

(The *turnstile* ('$\vdash$') marks the conclusion.) The proof:

(1)	$\sim$D $\lor$ E	A
(2)	$\sim$D $\rightarrow$ $\sim$E	A
(3)	D $\rightarrow$ E	1 AR
(4)	E $\rightarrow$ D	2 CN
(5)	D $\leftrightarrow$ E	3,4 $\leftrightarrow$I

The 'A' entries in the justification column identify lines 1 and 2 as premises of the argument. The third entry in the justification column is an abbreviation of 'Derived from line 1 by the Arrow Rule'.

Proofs in the second group employ the Arrow In, Tilde In, Tilde Out, or Wedge Out rules. Two kinds of assumptions occur in such proofs: *original* and *provisional* assumptions. The premises of the argument whose validity is being proven are the original assumptions. Additional assumptions are made to facilitate construction of the proof and then *discharged* before the proof is completed; these are provisional assumptions. Assumptions are discharged by the use of the four rules listed at the beginning of the paragraph. Proofs in this second group include a fourth column, the assumption-dependence column, located to the left of the line-number column. This column indicates for each statement in the proof which assumption(s) it depends upon. One purpose of the assumption-dependence column is to help indicate when a proof is complete. A proof is incomplete if the last line depends on any provisional assumptions.

For each of our eighteen inference rules we adopt a principle for determining the assumption dependence of any line introduced by that rule. These principles are stated in the chart below.

Assumption-Dependence Principles

→I	The conditional derived, $\mathcal{A} \rightarrow \mathcal{B}$, depends on whatever assumptions $\mathcal{B}$ depends on (less $\mathcal{A}$).
~I	The negation derived, $\sim\mathcal{A}$, depends on whatever assumptions $\mathcal{B}$ & $\sim\mathcal{B}$ depends on (less $\mathcal{A}$).
~O	The statement derived, $\mathcal{A}$, depends on whatever assumptions $\mathcal{B}$ & $\sim\mathcal{B}$ depends on (less $\sim\mathcal{A}$).
∨O	The statement derived, $\mathcal{C}$, depends on whatever assumptions $\mathcal{A} \vee \mathcal{B}$ depends on plus whatever $\mathcal{C}$ depends on in its derivation from $\mathcal{A}$ (less $\mathcal{A}$) plus whatever $\mathcal{C}$ depends on in its derivation from $\mathcal{B}$ (less $\mathcal{B}$).
the other 14 rules	The statement derived depends on all of the assumptions on which the premise(s) of the step depend(s). (We refer to this as the "standard assumption-dependence principle.")

An assumption (original or provisional) depends upon itself.

I illustrate the format for proofs in the second group by constructing several proofs.

F → G ⊢ (F & H) → G

1	(1)	F → G	A
2	(2)	F & H	PA
2	(3)	F	2 &O
1,2	(4)	G	1,3 →O
1	(5)	(F & H) → G	2–4 →I

The wff on line 2 is a provisional assumption (PA) made to facilitate the Arrow In step on line 5. The justification entry on line 5 is short for 'Derived by the Arrow In Rule from the derivation of line 4 from the assumption on line 2'. (The use of a hyphen rather than a comma in the justification entries for steps of Arrow In, Tilde In, Tilde Out, and Wedge Out is intended to distinguish these rules symbolically from the other fourteen inference rules.) Notice that lines 2 through 4 depend upon the provisional assumption, but that line 5 does not. Line 5 depends on whatever assumptions line 4 depends on (1 and 2) less assumption 2; hence it depends on 1. Only numbers of assumption lines can appear in the column on the left.

The Tilde Out Rule is used extensively in this volume. This proof illustrates its employment:

~I → I ⊢ I

1	(1)	~I → I	A
2	(2)	~I	PA
1,2	(3)	I	1,2 →O
1,2	(4)	I & ~I	3,2 &I
1	(5)	I	2–4 ~O

The justification entry on line 5 is an abbreviation of 'Derived by the Tilde Out Rule from the derivation of the standard contradiction[1] on line 4 from the assumption on line 2'. Although the conclusion of the argument is reached on line 3, the proof cannot be concluded at that point because line 3 depends on the provisional assumption.

The most complex of the eighteen rules is the Wedge Out Rule. The following proof indicates how this rule is applied.

J ∨ K, J → L, K → M ⊢ L ∨ M

1	(1)	J ∨ K	A
2	(2)	J → L	A

---

[1]A standard contradiction is a conjunction whose right conjunct is the negation of the left conjunct.

3	(3)	K → M	A
4	(4)	J	PA
2,4	(5)	L	2,4 →O
2,4	(6)	L ∨ M	5 ∨I
7	(7)	K	PA
3,7	(8)	M	3,7 →O
3,7	(9)	L ∨ M	8 ∨I
1,2,3	(10)	L ∨ M	1,4–6,7–9 ∨O

The entry in the justification column on line 10 is an abbreviation of 'Derived by the Wedge Out Rule from line 1, and the derivation of line 6 from the assumption on line 4, and the derivation of line 9 from the assumption on line 7'. Line 10 depends on whatever assumptions line 1 depends on (assumption 1); plus whatever assumptions line 6 depends on, discounting line 4 (assumption 2); plus whatever assumptions line 9 depends on, discounting line 7 (assumption 3). So, line 10 depends on assumptions 1 through 3.

For a full presentation of the material in this appendix, see Chapters One through Nine of my *Introduction to Logic: Propositional Logic.*

appendix two

An Expanded Set of Inference Rules

The set of inference rules developed in Chapters Three and Four does not include any quantifier "In" rules. In this appendix I expand the system by adding two such rules and strengthening the Quantifier Exchange Rule. The main virtue of the expanded system is that proofs in it tend to be shorter (by about four lines) than comparable proofs in the original system. The main drawback of the expanded system lies in the complexity of one of the new rules. Another drawback is that proofs in it are often more difficult to devise (even though shorter) than comparable proofs in the original system. The expanded set consists of EO, UO, and the following three rules:

> ### The [Strengthened] Quantifier Exchange Rule (QE):
>
> From $\sim(x)\mathcal{A}x$ derive $(\exists x)\sim\mathcal{A}x$ and vice versa.
> From $\sim(\exists x)\mathcal{A}x$ derive $(x)\sim\mathcal{A}x$ and vice versa.

> ### The Existential Quantifier In Rule (EI): Derive an existential quantification from any instance of it.

> ### The Universal Quantifier In Rule (UI): Derive a universal quantification from any instance of it, *provided that* the name being replaced by a variable does not occur in:

(1) the symbolization of the argument being tested,
(2) any line derived by EO above the universal quantification itself,
(3) any provisional assumption on which the instance depends, or
(4) the universal quantification itself.

These rules apply to whole lines only; they employ the standard assumption-dependence principle.

I illustrate the employment of the Existential Quantifier In Rule by constructing a proof for this argument:

(∃x)(Hx & Bx), (x)(Bx → Ix) ⊢ (∃x)(Hx & Ix)

(1)	(∃x)(Hx & Bx)	A
(2)	(x)(Bx → Ix)	A
(3)	Ha & Ba	1 EO
(4)	Ba → Ia	2 UO
(5)	Ba	3 &O
(6)	Ia	4,5 →O
(7)	Ha	3 &O
(8)	Ha & Ia	7,6 &I
(9)	(∃x)(Hx & Ix)	8 EI

You may wish to compare this proof with a proof for the same argument which does not employ EI; see p. 37.

I use the Universal Quantifier In Rule in a proof for this argument:

(x)(Hx → Gx), (x)(Gx → ~Ix) ⊢ (x)(Hx → ~Ix)

(1)	(x)(Hx → Gx)	A
(2)	(x)(Gx → ~Ix)	A
(3)	Ha → Ga	1 UO
(4)	Ga → ~Ia	2 UO
(5)	Ha → ~Ia	3,4 CH
(6)	(x)(Hx → ~Ix)	5 UI

Notice that the UI step satisfies the four restrictions on the rule. Compare this proof with a proof for the same argument on p. 37.

appendix three

Partial Solutions to Starred Exercises

Chapter Two

1. (c) (∃x)(Jx & ~Tx)
    (d) ~Dm
    (i) (∃x)(Bx & Ax)

2. (b) (x)(Px → ~Wx)
    (k) (x)(Ex → Dx)
    (m) (x)(Px → Gx)
    (p) (x)(Ex → Cx)
    (x) Lonely are the brave =
        The brave are lonely =
        (x)(Bx → Lx)

3. (c) All consumer advocates are activists.
        There are other acceptable translations.

Chapter Three

4. (b) (3) (x)(Fx → Dx)
        (4) Fe → De
        (5) De
        (6)   5,1 &I
        (7)   3-6 ~I

9. (1) Ka   A
    (2) (x)(Kx → ~Px)   A

(3) (x)(Dx → Px)   A
(4) Ka → ~Pa   2 UO
(5) Da → Pa   3 UO
(6) ~Pa   4,1 →O
(7) ~Da   5,6 MT
There are other correct proofs.

10. (a) (4) Ca → ~Na
       (5)   3 &O
       (6) ~Na
       (7) Na
       (8) Na & ~Na

12. (1) (x)(Mx → Sx)   A
     (2) (x)(Ax → ~Sx)   A
     (3) (∃x)(Ax & Mx)   PA
     (4)   3 EO
     (5)   1 UO
     (6)   2 UO
     (7) Ma   4 &O
     (8)   5,7 →O
     (9)   4 &O
     (10)   6,9 →O
     (11)   8,10 &I
     (12) ~(∃x)(Ax & Mx)   3–11 ~I

*Several wffs have been omitted from the above proof (and subsequent proofs); you should
supply them. The purpose of these omissions is to encourage you to engage in proof construction, rather than passively observing my work.*

Chapter Four

15. (a) (3) (∃x)~(Ax → Bx)
       (4) (x)~(Ax & ~Bx)
       (5)   3 EO
       (6) ~(Af & ~Bf)
       (7)   6 AR
       (8) (Af → Bf) & ~(Af → Bf)

16. (1) (x)(Ax → Bx)   A
     (2) (x)(Bx → Cx)   A
     (3)   PA
     (4)   3 QE
     (5)   4 EO
     (6)   1 UO
     (7)   2 UO
     (8)   6,7 CH
     (9)   8,5 &I
     (10) (x)(Ax → Cx)   3–9 ~O

19. (1) ~Ch   A
     (2) Eh   A
     (3)   PA
     (4)   3 QE
     (5)   4 UO
     (6) ~~Ch   5,2 CA
     (7)   1,6 &I
     (8) (∃x)(Ex & ~Cx)   3–7 ~O

Chapter Five

26. (f) (x)(Kx ↔ Yx)
    (h) (x)(Ox ↔ ~Fx)
    (n) (∃x)(Hx & Cx & Sx)
    (p) (x)[(Gx & Wx) → ~Bx]
    (s) (x)[Bx → (Fx ∨ Mx)]
    (u) (x)[Ax ↔ (Bx & Cx)]
    (x) (∃x)[Dx & Ux & (Lx → Hx)]

27. (b) Not everyone is obese.
    (e) A person is obese if and only if he isn't a vegetarian.

30. (1) ~(x)Kx   A
    (2) (x)(Hx → Kx)   A
    (3)   PA
    (4)   1 QE
    (5)   4 EO
    (6)   2 UO
    (7)   3 UO
    (8)   6,7 →O
    (9)   8,5 &I
    (10) ~(x)Hx   3–9 ~I

34. It is wrong to say that humans are the only animals that blush =
    It is false that all animals that blush are humans =
    ~(x)[(Ax & Bx) → Hx]
    [Note the difference in meaning between 'the only' and 'only'.]
    (1) (∃x)(Rx & Bx)   A
    (2) (x)[Rx → (~Hx & Ax)]   A
    (3)   PA
    (4)   1 EO
    (5)   2 UO
    (6)   3 UO
    (7) Ra   4 &O
    (8)   5,7 →O
    (9) ~Ha   8 &O
    (10)   6,9 MT
    (11)   4 &O
    (12)   10,11 CA
    (13)   8 &O
    (14)   13,12 &I
    (15) ~(x)[(Ax & Bx) → Hx]   3–14 ~I

39. (1) ~(Tm & Tw)   A
    (2)   PA
    (3)   2 QE
    (4) ~~Tm   3 UO
    (5)   4 DN
    (6)   1,5 CA
    (7)   3 UO
    (8)   6,7 &I
    (9) (∃x)~Tx   2–8 ~O
    A high-school sophomore (Bill Webber) constructed a correct eight-line proof for exercise 39. Can you?

Chapter Six

42. (b)

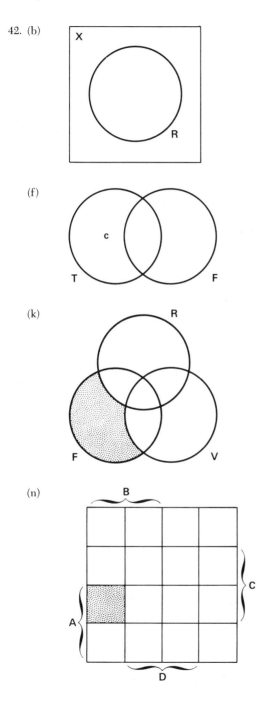

(f)

(k)

(n)

44. All *G* are *H*. *v* is *H*. So, *v* is *G*.   **invalid**

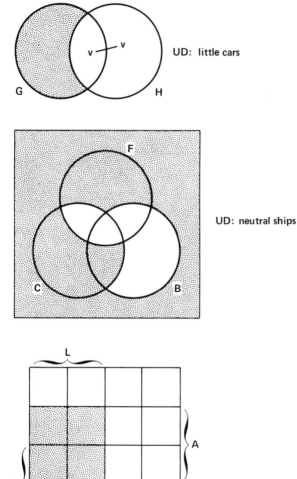

UD: little cars

52.   **valid**

UD: neutral ships

54.   **valid**

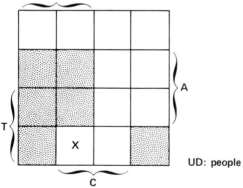

UD: people

Chapter Seven

56.

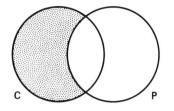

Needed existential premise: Conifers exist.

(1) (x)(Cx → Px)   A
(2) (∃x)Cx   A
(3)   PA
(4)   3 QE
(5)   2 EO
(6)   1 UO
(7)   4 UO
(8)   6,5 →O
(9)   7,5 CA
(10)   8,9 &I
(11) (∃x)(Cx & Px)   3–10 ~O

Chapter Eight

60. (b) ~(∃x)Ux → (x)(Ux → Bx)
         Also correct: (x)~Ux → (x)(Ux → Bx)
    (g) (∃x)(Ix & Mx) → (x)(Ax → Dx)
    (n) (∃x)(Sx & Ex) & (∃x)(Sx & ~Ex)

61. (c) If there is something nonphysical, then something mental exists.

62. (a) 2   (2)   (∃x)~Bx
         3   (3)   (x)Ax
         2   (4)   ~Ba
         1   (5)   Aa→ Ba
         3   (6)   Aa
         1,3   (7)   Ba
         1,2,3   (8)   Ba & ~Ba
         1,2   (9)   ~(x)Ax
         1   (10)

64.

1	(1)	(∃x)(Lx & Wx)	A
2	(2)	~(∃x)Lx	PA
2	(3)		2 QE
1	(4)		1 EO
2	(5)		3 UO
1	(6)		4 &O
1,2	(7)		6,5 &I
1	(8)	(∃x)Lx	2–7 ~O
9	(9)		PA
9	(10)		9 QE
9	(11)		10 UO
1	(12)		4 &O
1,9	(13)		12,11 &I
1	(14)	(∃x)Wx	9–13 ~O
1	(15)	(∃x)Lx & (∃x)Wx	8,14 &I

67.

1	(1)	(x)Dx	A
2	(2)		PA
3	(3)	(∃x)Tx	PA
3	(4)		3 EO
1	(5)		1 UO
2	(6)		2 UO
1,2	(7)		6,5 →O
1,2,3	(8)		4,7 &I
1,2	(9)		3–8 ~I
1	(10)	(x)(Dx → ~Tx) → ~(∃x)Tx	2–9 →I

Chapter Nine

74. ~(x)(Cx → Ix) ⊢ (x)(Cx → ~Ix)

UD: people

Cx = x is a Protestant
Ix = x is a Lutheran

It is false that all Protestants are Lutherans. (T)
So, no Protestants are Lutherans. (F)

77. (x)(Rx → Ax) ⊢ (x)[(Mx & ~Rx) → ~Ax]

UD: animals

Rx = x is a collie
Ax = x is a dog
Mx = x is brown

All collies are dogs. (T)
So, no brown non-collies are dogs. (F)

82. (x)(Sx ∨ Wx) ⊢ (x)Sx ∨ (x)Wx

UD: positive integers

Sx = x is even
Wx = x is odd

Each positive integer is even or odd. (T)
So, either all positive integers are even or all are odd. (F)

Chapter Ten

83. (d) (∃x)[Px & (y)(Sy → ~Kxy)]
        Also correct: (∃x)[Px & ~(∃y)(Sy & Kxy)]

84. (d) There is a teacher who is bored by every student.

87. (d) ~(∃x)(y)Pxy
        Also correct: (x)~(y)Pxy
        Also correct: (x)(∃y)~Pxy
    (j) (x)(y)[(Sx & Hyx) → Sy]
        Also correct: (x)[Sx → (y)(Hyx → Sy)]
    (l) (x)(y)[(~Kx & Ky) → Fxy]
    (m) (x)[(∃y)(Wy & Byx & Lx) → Ax]
        Also correct: (x)(y)[(Wx & Bxy & Ly) → Ay]
        [*Note: Bxy = x* bites *y* (not *x* is bitten by *y*).]

Chapter Eleven

88. (a) (2) ~(∃x)(∃y)Rxy
         (3) (x)(y)~Rxy
         (4) ~Rab
         (5) Rab & ~Rab

90. (1) (x)(Ox → ~Mrx) & Mrd   A
    (2)   1 &O
    (3) Od → ~Mrd   2 UO
    (4)   1 &O
    (5)   3 CN
    (6) ~Od   5,4 →O

93. (1) (x)Ixx   A
    (2) ~(x)Exx   A
    (3)   PA
    (4)   2 QE
    (5) ~Eaa   4 EO
    (6) Iaa   1 UO
    (7) Iaa → Eaa   3 UO
    (8)   7,6 →O
    (9)   8,5 &I
    (10) ~(x)(y)(Ixy → Exy)   3-9 ~I

96. 1   (1) (x)(y)(Sxy → Rxy)   A
    2   (2)   PA
    3   (3) ~(∃x)(Bx & Rax)   PA
    3   (4)   3 QE
    2   (5) Bb & Sab   2 EO
    1   (6) Sab → Rab   1 UO
    3   (7) ~(Bb & Rab)   4 UO
    2   (8) Sab   5 &O
    1,2   (9)   6,8 →O
    1,2,3 (10)   7,9 CA

2	(11)		5 &O
1,2,3	(12)		11,10 &I
1,2	(13)		3–12 ~O
1	(14)	$(\exists x)(Bx$ & $Sax) \rightarrow (\exists x)(Bx$ & $Rax)$	2–13 →I

102.	(1)	$(x)(Rx \rightarrow Jx)$	A
	(2)		PA
	(3)		2 QE
	(4)		3 EO
	(5)	Pa & $(\exists y)(Ry$ & $Lay)$ & $\sim(\exists y)(Jy$ & $Lay)$	4 AR
	(6)	$(\exists y)(Ry$ & $Lay)$	5 &O
	(7)	$\sim(\exists y)(Jy$ & $Lay)$	5 &O
	(8)		7 QE
	(9)	Rb & Lab	6 EO
	(10)		1 UO
	(11)		8 UO
	(12)	Rb	9 &O
	(13)		10,12 →O
	(14)		11,13 CA
	(15)		9 &O
	(16)		15,14 &I
	(17)	$(x)\{[Px$ & $(\exists y)(Ry$ & $Lxy)] \rightarrow (\exists y)(Jy$ & $Lxy)\}$	2–16 ~O

107. $(\exists x)(\exists y)(Pxy$ & $\sim Cxy) \vdash \sim(x)(y)(Cxy \rightarrow Pxy)$

UD: people

$Pxy = x$ is a parent of y
$Cxy = x$ is mother of y

Someone is a parent of a second person, but not mother of that person.   (T)

So, it is false that each mother of a person is a parent of that person. [*Restated:* There is a mother of some person who is not a parent of that person.]   (F)

111. $(\exists x)(\exists y)(Okxy$ & $Ogxy), (\exists x)(Okhx \lor Oghx) \vdash (\exists x)(Okhx$ & $Oghx.)$

[*Note:* The second premise may also be symbolized: $(\exists x)Okhx \lor (\exists x)Oghx$]

UD: U.S. cities

$Oxyz = x$ is between y and z
$k =$ Des Moines
$g =$ Cleveland
$h =$ Chicago

There are two cities between which lie Des Moines and Cleveland (San Jose and New York City, for instance).   (T)

There is a city such that either Des Moines or Cleveland is between Chicago and it (San Jose).   (T)

So, there is a city such that both Des Moines and Cleveland are between Chicago and it.   (F)

Index

The Ten Primitive Propositional Inference Rules

	IN	OUT
→	From the derivation of $\mathcal{B}$ from assumption $\mathcal{A}$ (and perhaps other assumptions) derive $\mathcal{A} \rightarrow \mathcal{B}$.	From $\mathcal{A} \rightarrow \mathcal{B}$ and $\mathcal{A}$ derive $\mathcal{B}$.
&	From $\mathcal{A}$ and $\mathcal{B}$ derive $\mathcal{A} \& \mathcal{B}$.	From $\mathcal{A} \& \mathcal{B}$ derive either $\mathcal{A}$ or $\mathcal{B}$.
∨	From $\mathcal{A}$ derive either $\mathcal{A} \vee \mathcal{B}$ or $\mathcal{B} \vee \mathcal{A}$.	From $\mathcal{A} \vee \mathcal{B}$, $\mathcal{A} \rightarrow \mathcal{C}$, and $\mathcal{B} \rightarrow \mathcal{C}$ derive $\mathcal{C}$.
↔	From $\mathcal{A} \rightarrow \mathcal{B}$ and $\mathcal{B} \rightarrow \mathcal{A}$ derive $\mathcal{A} \leftrightarrow \mathcal{B}$.	From $\mathcal{A} \leftrightarrow \mathcal{B}$ derive either $\mathcal{A} \rightarrow \mathcal{B}$ or $\mathcal{B} \rightarrow \mathcal{A}$.
~	From the derivation of $\mathcal{B} \& \sim\mathcal{B}$ from assumption $\mathcal{A}$ (and perhaps other assumptions) derive $\sim\mathcal{A}$.	From the derivation of $\mathcal{B} \& \sim\mathcal{B}$ from assumption $\sim\mathcal{A}$ (and perhaps other assumptions) derive $\mathcal{A}$.

The Eight Derived Propositional Inference Rules

Modus Tollens (MT)	From $\mathcal{A} \rightarrow \mathcal{B}$ and $\sim \mathcal{B}$ derive $\sim \mathcal{A}$.
Disjunctive Argument (DA)	From $\mathcal{A} \vee \mathcal{B}$ and $\sim \mathcal{A}$ derive $\mathcal{B}$. From $\mathcal{A} \vee \mathcal{B}$ and $\sim \mathcal{B}$ derive $\mathcal{A}$.
Conjunctive Argument (CA)	From $\sim(\mathcal{A} \& \mathcal{B})$ and $\mathcal{A}$ derive $\sim \mathcal{B}$. From $\sim(\mathcal{A} \& \mathcal{B})$ and $\mathcal{B}$ derive $\sim \mathcal{A}$.
Chain Argument (CH)	From $\mathcal{A} \rightarrow \mathcal{B}$ and $\mathcal{B} \rightarrow \mathcal{C}$ derive $\mathcal{A} \rightarrow \mathcal{C}$.
Double Negation (DN)	From $\mathcal{A}$ derive $\sim\sim \mathcal{A}$ and vice versa.
DeMorgan's Law (DM)	From $\mathcal{A} \& \mathcal{B}$ derive $\sim(\sim \mathcal{A} \vee \sim \mathcal{B})$ and vice versa. From $\sim(\mathcal{A} \& \mathcal{B})$ derive $\sim \mathcal{A} \vee \sim \mathcal{B}$ and vice versa. From $\sim \mathcal{A} \& \sim \mathcal{B}$ derive $\sim(\mathcal{A} \vee \mathcal{B})$ and vice versa. From $\sim(\sim \mathcal{A} \& \sim \mathcal{B})$ derive $\mathcal{A} \vee \mathcal{B}$ and vice versa.
Arrow (AR)	From $\mathcal{A} \rightarrow \mathcal{B}$ derive $\sim \mathcal{A} \vee \mathcal{B}$ and vice versa. From $\sim \mathcal{A} \rightarrow \mathcal{B}$ derive $\mathcal{A} \vee \mathcal{B}$ and vice versa. From $\mathcal{A} \rightarrow \mathcal{B}$ derive $\sim(\mathcal{A} \& \sim \mathcal{B})$ and vice versa. From $\sim(\mathcal{A} \rightarrow \mathcal{B})$ derive $\mathcal{A} \& \sim \mathcal{B}$ and vice versa.
Contra-position (CN)	From $\mathcal{A} \rightarrow \mathcal{B}$ derive $\sim \mathcal{B} \rightarrow \sim \mathcal{A}$ and vice versa. From $\mathcal{A} \rightarrow \sim \mathcal{B}$ derive $\mathcal{B} \rightarrow \sim \mathcal{A}$. From $\sim \mathcal{A} \rightarrow \mathcal{B}$ derive $\sim \mathcal{B} \rightarrow \mathcal{A}$.

The Three Predicate Inference Rules

Universal Quantifier Out (UO)	From a universal quantification derive any instance of it.
Existential Quantifier Out (EO)	From an existential quantification derive any instance of it, *provided that* the name being introduced does not occur in the symbolization of the argument being tested or on any line above the line derived.
Quantifier Exchange (QE)	From $\sim(x)\mathcal{A}x$ derive $(\exists x)\sim\mathcal{A}x$. From $\sim(\exists x)\mathcal{A}x$ derive $(x)\sim\mathcal{A}x$.